AP®
U.S. History
Prep

D1545293

WILEY

AP® U.S. History Prep

Jonathan Chu

Warren Hierl

Louisa Moffitt

Bill Shelton

AP® is a trademark registered by the College Board, which is not affiliated with, and does not endorse, this product

WILEY

Cover Image: © DHuss/Gettyimages

Cover Design: Wiley

Copyright © 2020 by John Wiley & Sons, Inc. All rights reserved.

Published by John Wiley & Sons, Inc., Hoboken, New Jersey.

Published simultaneously in Canada.

No part of this publication may be reproduced, stored in a retrieval system, or transmitted in any form or by any means, electronic, mechanical, photocopying, recording, scanning, or otherwise, except as permitted under Section 107 or 108 of the 1976 United States Copyright Act, without either the prior written permission of the Publisher, or authorization through payment of the appropriate per-copy fee to the Copyright Clearance Center, Inc., 222 Rosewood Drive, Danvers, MA 01923, (978) 750-8400, fax (978) 646-8600, or on the Web at www.copyright.com. Requests to the Publisher for permission should be addressed to the Permissions Department, John Wiley & Sons, Inc., 111 River Street, Hoboken, NJ 07030, (201) 748-6011, fax (201) 748-6008, or online at http://www.wiley.com/go/permissions.

Limit of Liability/Disclaimer of Warranty: While the publisher and author have used their best efforts in preparing this book, they make no representations or warranties with respect to the accuracy or completeness of the contents of this book and specifically disclaim any implied warranties of merchantability or fitness for a particular purpose. No warranty may be created or extended by sales representatives or written sales materials. The advice and strategies contained herein may not be suitable for your situation. You should consult with a professional where appropriate. Neither the publisher nor author shall be liable for any loss of profit or any other commercial damages, including but not limited to special, incidental, consequential, or other damages.

For general information on our other products and services or for technical support, please contact our Customer Care Department within the United States at (800) 762-2974, outside the United States at (317) 572-3993 or fax (317) 572-4002.

Wiley publishes in a variety of print and electronic formats and by print-on-demand. Some material included with standard print versions of this book may not be included in e-books or in print-on-demand. If this book refers to media such as a CD or DVD that is not included in the version you purchased, you may download this material at http://booksupport.wiley.com. For more information about Wiley products, visit www.wiley.com.

ISBN 978-1-119-68251-6

Printed in the United States of America

V406696_022420

Contents

CONTENTS

Preface

AP U.S. History Prep is a study guide that provides sample questions drafted by experienced APUSH teachers, test developers, consultants, and readers to help you develop the disciplinary habits of mind and reasoning skills essential to historical understanding and success on the APUSH exam. Aligned with the learning objectives, historical content, and guidelines of the APUSH curriculum and collegiate-level survey courses, this guide introduces you to the different question types found on the exam: multiple-choice, document-based, long essay, and short-answer. To help you prepare for success, *AP U.S. History Prep* is unique in explaining how responses are aligned to scoring rubrics.

Jonathan M. Chu holds a PhD from the University of Washington and is a professor at the University of Massachusetts, Boston and editor of *The New England Quarterly*. A specialist in early American history, he has written on seventeenth century religious dissent and on the economic impact of the American Revolution. He participated in the APUSH Reading in various positions and served as chair of the Test Development Committee and Chief Reader.

Warren Hierl taught AP U.S. History at the Career Center in Winston-Salem, NC, for thirty-eight years. An original member of the College Board AP Social Studies Vertical Teams Guide Committee, he has conducted AP workshops, Summer Institutes, and pre-AP workshops. He has been a reader, table, exam, and, for ten years, the question leader on the DBQ. He is currently a College Board APUSH consultant, and member of the College Board's Pre-AP National Faculty.

Louisa Moffitt holds a DAST from Emory University and a PhD from Georgia State University, has taught AP U.S. History at the Marist School for the past thirty-three years, and served as reader, table, question, and exam leader, and as Assistant Chief Reader. In addition, she has been a member of the Test Development Committee and a College Board consultant and national mentor for the AP U.S. History program.

Bill Shelton holds a PhD from the University of Kentucky and has taught AP U.S. History for thirty-nine years; the last thirty-four at Trinity Valley School in Fort Worth. He has served as a reader, table, and exam leader and was the Assistant Chief Reader responsible for the introduction of the onsite and online scoring of the short-answer questions. He co-chaired the Test Development Committee and is a College Board consultant for workshops and institutes throughout the United States and China.

CHAPTER ONE

Welcome to AP U.S. History Prep

APUSH and the College Survey

Welcome to **AP U.S. History Prep.** As experienced teachers, test developers, and scorers or graders of the written portions of the exam, we designed this text to help you with APUSH by providing questions similar to those used on the exam and suggesting strategies for answering them. We have set this book up to guide you through your preparation for the APUSH exam in May.

In writing this text, we want you to be rigorous, deliberate, and thoughtful about learning history. In asking that you reflect on your responses when you take the Instructional Exam and the Practice Exams, we want you to get the answers and essays right, but we also want you to improve your habits of mind and historical thinking and reasoning skills because we believe those will reinforce your content learning and better prepare you for the exam.

Central to the construction of our questions and our commentary is our alignment of **AP U.S. History Prep** with the learning objectives of the 2019 *AP U.S. History Course and Exam Description*. As with APUSH, our approach has been to provide questions and supporting materials that cover the significant events, individuals, and historical developments and themes of U.S. history from 1491 to the present. AP U.S. History Prep replicates the historical thinking processes and reasoning found in a two-semester college or university survey. We have structured this book to help you build skills—habits of historical thinking—in preparation for the study of history and to provide practical advice on how to approach answering the different kinds of questions you will face on the exam.

Our purpose with **AP U.S. History Prep** is, like the College Board's, to provide you not only with the knowledge and skills you will need to earn college credit or placement but with an introduction to the habits of mind necessary for beginning students of history. Although the College Board conducts occasional surveys to determine what constitutes the content of the typical U.S. history course, the *AP U.S. History Course and Exam Description* provides no exhaustive, common list of names, dates, and events to study. While history teachers recognize that the course cannot be taught without careful attention to a common core of events, individuals, developments and themes, they are free to choose what historical materials they wish to teach. The reason for this—aside from the fact that no two university-level surveys are exactly alike, prompting the observation that making all professors do the same thing is like herding cats—is that each historian has unique perspectives on content and themes, assesses the significance of events differently, or just prefers to focus on some topics rather than others. Operating from an unstated but presumably shared consensus, U.S. historians generally will agree on the major landmarks of the survey—the Columbian Exchange, European colonization, the American Revolution, antebellum reforms, technological change, the Civil War, the Gilded Age, the Progressive Era, the Great Depression, Civil Rights, the resurgence of Conservatism, and others. Because university instructors have unique interests and because they have greater discretion than high school instructors in their choice of materials and subjects, an individual instructor may choose to approach signature topics differently. Some, for example, focus more on Native Americans' resistance to European settlement than on the structures of colonial settlement. Some may document changes in financial regulation instead of focusing on the construction of massive public works projects during the Great Depression. This does not mean students have to learn fewer facts about events, individuals, or historical developments; without question, the more details you know about the history of America, the better off you will be. As with foreign languages, the more vocabulary you know, the easier it will be to express yourself. It's a lot easier to get the meal you want in Paris if you know the French names for the food on the menu. In addition, the lack of prescribed content allows teachers the flexibility to present material that, in their best judgment, will develop students' historical thinking skills and reasoning processes and better prepare them with a deeper understanding of the history of the United States.

The APUSH course, in place of just memorizing facts, requires greater emphasis on developing the processes of historical thinking and reasoning, and writing to reflect the learning objectives found in university surveys. By reducing the breadth of factual information, the course framework encourages teachers to select historical content appropriate to their classroom to teach a deep understanding of the nature of change over time. The aim is to teach students to analyze and explain rather than merely to memorize information. To encourage deeper study and understanding of historic events, the course framework also gives teachers more latitude to use content that they know would be more interesting for their students. The structure of the exam attempts to assess students' historical thinking and reasoning by balancing the knowledge of content with skills that require the comprehension of historical images and data, the analysis of documents, and the ability to explain and communicate one's understandings.

This book will immerse you in the testing world of APUSH. Chapter 2 charts how APUSH testing assesses historical thinking and reasoning skills, the organization of historical themes, and content knowledge while providing information on how the test is scored and how to use the instructional and sample tests. Chapter 3 includes an Instructional Exam with a detailed breakdown of how to approach the different types of questions. Chapter 4 consists of two Practice Exams, and Chapter 5 provides some last-minute suggestions for doing your best. In addition, you can access 500 multiple-choice questions (MCQs) online using the scratch-off PIN provided on the inside front cover of this book.

APUSH has four different categories of questions: fifty-five multiple-choice questions (MCQs), four short-answer questions (SAQs), a document-based question (DBQ), and a long essay question (LEQ). The MCQs require skills developed during the year of study that demonstrate your ability to combine specific content knowledge with deeper understandings of events, individuals, or historical developments. Test developers design MCQs so that knowing the answer (called the key) requires connecting the information in a text or image (called a stimulus) to some historical fact. The questions are framed so that they are not dependent on a single, specific detail but rather can be answered with material over the broad chronology of American history from 1491 to the present that your teacher has selected for your AP class. The SAQs ask you to connect material you have studied to larger historical themes or developments. They are essentially identifications asking you to provide a fact or brief explanation of significance that responds to the prompt or question. The traditional DBQ and the LEQ are exercises intended to assess your historical reasoning and writing skills. On the LEQ, scorers assess test takers' ability to write historical arguments on a specific subject. On the DBQ, scorers evaluate test takers' ability to read and analyze documents and use them in the development of an historical argument.

APUSH tries to be give teachers discretion in their selection factual material while seeking to cover the material of a customary college survey. It wants your teachers to use materials interesting to you as young historians. Thus, it allows you to provide your own historically accurate detail in explaining a larger development or theme rather than one specifically designated by the test developers—being able to use the tea duties rather than the Stamp Act as an example of legislation that caused the American Revolution. This is especially true of the LEQs and SAQs; as you review the sample essays and SAQs, note that they do not necessarily have a single correct response; rather, like the APUSH course guidelines and the exam, they allow you to use the content you have already learned to support your answers. For example, you are less likely to be required to identify a narrow, specific fact, such as the Pequot War, and more likely to be able to use King Philip's War or the Pueblo Revolt as alternatives to answer a question on the nature of the early interaction of Native people and European colonial settlers. This approach also encourages instruction that is more consistent with the skills and habits of mind that are more useful in higher education history classes.

Historians' Habits of Mind

What the College Board defines as "Historical Thinking Skills and Reasoning Processes," we sum up as "habits of mind." Our approach in our own teaching is less on emphasizing memorization of factual information and more on understanding the big picture, and we suggest that as you approach your studies, you try to think about history as patterns of related facts until they literally become habits. Having an historians' habits of mind has a practical APUSH purpose. We believe that by approaching content knowledge with active habits of mind, by observing and thinking about events, individuals, and developments historically and in the bigger picture, you will be more apt to better remember facts while understanding more deeply the ebb and flow of history. These habits of mind also makes your factual knowledge more useful when you are able to connect varying content across time and use it to illuminate and explain multiple themes—in brief, to be better able to explain and analyze and to score higher on AP essays. As will become apparent in the commentary we attach to the question keys, these habits of mind can make for more sophisticated, complex essays that satisfy the generic rubric guides for those who score the Free Response Section (the SAQs, DBQs, and LFQs) of the APUSH exam.

Concerned with the study of changes over time in human societies, historians have developed habits of inquiry that allow them to examine historical facts and use them to illustrate and explain different themes. The *APUS History Course and Exam Description* lists eight essential themes:

1. American and National Identity (NAT)

2. Work, Exchange, and Technology (WXT)

3. Geography and the Environment (GEO)

4. Migration and Settlement (MIG)

5. Politics and Power (PCE)

6. America in the World (WOR)

7. American and Regional Culture (ARC)

8. Social Structures (SOC)

In studying history, many events, individuals, and developments overlap. Facts are frequently used in multiple circumstances, periods, and themes because historical events are complicated. Historians organize facts into themes or periods to help them think analytically about the stuff of history; they compare and contrast facts, establish connections, and determine continuities or changes over time to explain causation and shed light on consequences. For example, the circumstances of Andrew Carnegie's life can serve as an example of multiple themes and periods. An immigrant who transformed the application of technology to the manufacture of steel, Carnegie represented the impact of massive wealth on society and politics, the rise of monopolies and their regulation, and Gilded Age culture. Thus, Carnegie might be used in questions related to Work, Exchange, and Technology; American and Regional Culture; and Social Structures.

Historians begin their own work by describing events and trying to make sense of them. They ask what are familiar if not instinctive questions: what, where, and when an event happened and who was involved. Much of this process should already be familiar to you: It is what your teachers ask when they want to see if you know who James Madison was and what he wrote in *Federalist 10*. The next more difficult, but not entirely separate, step is to explain or analyze *Federalist 10*. To analyze, rather than describe, historians ask the explanatory questions why or how things happened. In *Federalist 10* Madison described how the Constitution checked the acquisition of power in government by balancing men's self-interests against those of others (the fact or description). Madison's goal was to convince the opponents of ratification that the centralization of power in the new Constitution would not lead to tyranny and was not dangerous (the why). Perhaps the most difficult question to answer is "so what?" or "why should we care?" because it builds on the knowledge of knowing who, what, when, and why. The significance of *Federalist 10* in this instance is its representation of the central principle of checks and balances in the constitutional government in the United States as an example of originalist intent. The last step, the "so what" question, is difficult, because it requires sophisticated thinking and an understanding of how events are connected; such thinking most likely will lead to higher scores on APUSH essays.

To determine the answers to analytical questions, historians employ a series of techniques unique to the study of the past, similar to what the course framework calls Reasoning Processes. First and foremost, historians try to determine the extent to which past events or developments have common characteristics (Comparison), are linked (Causation), or reflect patterns (Continuity and Change). In all three of these categories of inquiry, historians contextualize events or historical developments by looking at other events and developments to determine similarities or contrasts, causes or consequences, or a continuation with or departure from the past. One difficulty with trying to guide you through these habits of inquiry is that history is a fact-based discipline and, as in the television quiz show *Jeopardy!*, the answers (the facts about the events, individuals, or themes) are already given. You have to learn to ask the questions that can lead you to other events or developments and in turn enable you to compare and contextualize them and provide analytical explanations of causation, continuity, consequences, and significance.

Take, for example, a teacher who chooses to focus in detail on the Stamp Act when explaining the causes of the American Revolution. An understanding of the Stamp Act and its significance in American history begins with the knowledge of its details and its immediate context. Initiated in 1765 as part of the attempt to pay for Britain's massive war debt, the Stamp Act was a tax on newspapers, legal documents, and other commercial paper. The colonial protests including the destruction of the home of Thomas Hutchinson, Massachusetts' lieutenant governor, and the meeting of the Stamp Act Congress, marked the first events that led to the American Revolution. How your teacher presents the Stamp Act can provide the links when studying other events leading up to the Revolution.

- **Comparison:** What are other significant events leading to the Revolution?
  - The Boston Massacre
  - The Boston Tea Party
  - Stamp Act Riots in Philadelphia
  - Virginia's Stamp Act Resolves
- **Causation:** In what ways did the above events contribute to the coming of the Revolution?
  - Resolutions claiming rights of Englishmen: claims for more direct representation
  - Popular protests and boycotts
  - Fear of Parliament's policies in North America
- **Continuity and Change:** To what extent did the events leading up to the Revolution affect the writing of the Constitution?
  - **Continuity:**
    - The Constitution's preservation of rights (Bill of Rights)
    - The Constitution's provision for checking and balancing power (*Federalist 10*, Senate, Congress, and separate executive and judiciary)
    - The Constitution's provision for the representation of states (Senate) and persons (House of Representatives)
    - The Constitution's protection of the institution of slavery (Three-fifths clause, continuation of the slave trade until at least 1808)
  - **Change:**
    - The rise of political parties (Federalists and Democratic-Republicans, the first party systems)
    - The abolition of slavery (Congressional authorization to end the slave trade after 1808. [note here how the same fact can serve two explanatory purposes], Thirteenth Amendment)
    - The extension of the right to vote to women (Nineteenth Amendment)

As you review this analysis process, you should note that our example in moving from the description of the Stamp Act into a discussion of rights followed the analytical or explanatory thread along the theme Politics and Power (PCE); by slightly altering the nature of our inquiry, the discussion could equally have followed an alternative thematic unity of Social Structures (SOC):

- **Causation:** To what extent did the American Revolution alter the social structure of the United States?
  - Fear of Parliament's denial of rights
  - Popular protest and boycotts during the period 1765 to 1774
  - The Declaration of Independence
  - Claims for representation leading to an increased awareness of social inequality

- **Continuity and Change:** To what extent did the social structure change?
  - **Continuity:**
    - The protection of slavery by the Constitution
    - Voting rights based upon property holding
    - Some states' requirements for higher property qualifications for elected officials.
  - **Change:**
    - Growth of political democracy (expansion to universal white male suffrage)
    - Rise of political parties (Democratic-Republican Party)
    - Rise of the abolitionist movement
    - Women's participation in the Revolution leading to appeal for expanded social roles (Republican motherhood)

The shift taking place in our inquiry above happens when reflecting on the different circumstances in which a fact can be placed—that is to say how it is contextualized. Moving from description (recitation of facts) to analysis and explanation depends on seeing patterns of events or connections across themes. Themes are the connections that allow you to make comparisons across periods, see similarities and differences, and ask questions about the nature of the continuities and changes. How well you understand the multiple aspects, the different impacts, or the significance of facts is determined by the depth of your understanding of individual events or historical developments. While not all facts are comparable—remember, contrasts also are a form of conceptual link—it is the habit of reflection that enables you to move beyond description to analysis and explanation.

One final note on contextualization and significance: The determination of context and significance is an argument made and defended, not a correct or incorrect statement. Making a case for placing a fact in a specific, historically verifiable context or asserting its significance depends on how you present the case, the key to which is knowing the appropriate facts and being able to point to how those facts support your explanation or argument. Contextualizing or integrating historical events, individuals, or developments into the larger themes is the most sophisticated analytical skill that you can learn in the study of American history. The Stamp Act becomes significant to an argument about the causes of the American Revolution when you, the historian, place it in a context or argument that links it to a particular theme in explaining some aspect of the Revolution. Using a different theme—American and National Identity (NAT), Politics and Power (PCE), or Social Structures (SOC)—leads to different approaches and different uses of an event like the Stamp Act. An essay on national identity (NAT) might focus less on the protests and more on discussions on ideas expressing claims to rights or describing not what the protests did (trashing Thomas Hutchinson's house) but how they expanded political participation to a broader base of Americans (people who were not able to vote). An essay responding to questions of Politics and Power (PCE) would look at the way in which reaction against the Stamp Act represented the organization of the protests from the passing of Stamp Act Resolves to the convening of the Stamp Act Congress. Such an essay might spend more time discussing how crowd protests that involved trashing Thomas Hutchinson's and Andrew Oliver's houses intimidated tax collectors. The keys to learning to contextualize and synthesize are knowing content well and understanding it enough to be able to use facts in multiple contexts.

Critical Apparatus

As you exercise analytical skills, you also need to be aware of the ways in which sources shape our understandings of the past. One of history's great gifts is its inherent suspicion of appearances. This is especially true of the claims of evidence and documents you will encounter in your APUSH studies. Knowing the point of view, purpose, intended audience, and historical circumstances of documents will enable you to have a better sense of how to use them when responding to questions. If you can account for the ways in which the context of documents influences the information and arguments they provide us, your ability to explain events will not only come more easily, but your argument will be more effective and complex, resulting in higher scores.

In many ways, describing an historians' habits of mind is more difficult than actually practicing them. As you engage with America's past, you should constantly ask how the stories are linked, how one set of facts is connected to others. Trying to explain these connections will inevitably lead you to a better recall of those facts, a deeper understanding of themes and of historical change, and, we think, a higher APUSH score.

CHAPTER TWO

The Advanced Placement History Course

Designed to model the college survey U.S. history course, APUSH de-emphasizes rote memorization of selected facts and encourages a more balanced approach aimed at the acquisition of analytical and writing skills. Like its college counterpart, APUSH integrates content knowledge and historical thinking and reasoning skills. In *AP U.S. History: Course Guide and Exam Description*, the official course framework, you will find a detailed description of the content and skills you will need for the end-of-the-year exam. What follows here is our collective translation of the *Course Guide* to a more practical guide to learning these skills through a process we call an historians' habits of mind. Just as with sports, math, or learning a foreign language, learning history requires practice and the accumulation of knowledge. Learning history is the study (the practice) of history, the content knowledge, in a manner that leads to an understanding and application of the dynamics of historical change. More immediately, learning history will give you the ability to engage new factual information and be able to explain and analyze its connections to the sweep of U.S. history. Such an approach, we believe, is better suited to helping you to remember historical content; more important, as a practical matter, it will stand you in better stead on the APUSH exam and in future college coursework.

APUSH is structured for you to acquire historical thinking and reasoning skills while learning the content of the history of the United States from 1491, pre-European contact America, to the present over the course of the school year. To explain the historical thinking and reasoning skills and provide a common base of historical content knowledge, the *Course Guide and Exam Description* divides U.S. history into nine periods and eight themes. How historians divide American history into time periods—a process called periodization—and themes varies based on content or an individual historians' interpretation of connections and significance. While APUSH does not provide labels for the nine periods, we label them because doing so will help you remember details and place events in context. Labels for periodization in textbooks vary— usually they are the titles of chapters or sections that indicate the authors' approach to the broad sweep of American history—but the time periods are roughly the same. The application of different labels to periods reflects different big-picture interpretations or approaches to the content. In their application of historical thinking and reasoning skills, historians may observe patterns of connection that lead them to group events differently. For example, ending Period 2 and beginning Period 3 in 1754 means that APUSH sees the Seven Years' War as the beginning of the American Revolution and the independence of the United States. Another textbook might begin its discussion of the Revolution in 1763. The causes for the differences are subtle and, on the whole, largely ones of perspective. Because textbook authors might look at conditions arising during Seven Years' War as causing the Revolution, they would prefer to end the period of American colonial development in 1754; other authors who see the end of the struggles of France and Britain for supremacy in North America as the conclusion of a stage in colonial development would emphasize understanding the Revolution as a reaction to British policies occurring after 1763, the end of the Seven Years' War. The variation does not reflect a different understanding of the place of the Seven Years' War in causing the Revolution but reflects a degree of emphasis when explaining this particular moment in American history. This small distinction shows how factual information can serve multiple explanations, analyses, and themes. Thinking about how factual information can fit into different historical places— knowing that the history of Hull House can help explain the role of women and the state of the cities during the Progressive Era—deepens your historical understanding and has the practical advantage of making it easier for you to remember facts and to be able to use them in response to different questions.

APUSH Periods

Periods	Likely Exam Coverage %
Period 1: 1491–1607: Native American Societies and European Contact and Settlement	4–6%
Period 2: 1607–1754: Colonization of British North America	6–8%
Period 3: 1754–1800: Revolutionary America and the Early Republic	10–17%
Period 4: 1800–1848: The Market Revolution	10–17%
Period 5: 1844–1877: The Rise of Sectionalism and Civil War	10–17%
Period 6: 1877-1898: The Consequences of Industrialization	10–17%
Period: 7: 1890–1945: Domestic and Global Challenges	10–17%
Period 8: 1945–1980: Liberalism and Modernity	10–17%
Period 9: 1980–Present: International and Domestic Challenges	4–6%

Notice also how APUSH assigns percentages of questions to all periods with the least coverage assigned to Periods 1 and 9. The number of questions drawn from the different periods reinforces APUSH's intention not to specify the events, processes, or historical developments that must be studied. The College Board limits the breadth of coverage needed to teach the course so as to make it manageable for your teachers while insuring a common base of content knowledge. Limited content is drawn from Periods 1 and 9 for practical testing reasons. The history of pre-European contact, for example, is much too vast in chronology and subject matter to ensure that every teacher cover the same events in-depth. By starting Period 1 in 1491, APUSH limits the focus of content to the moment of European discovery and settlement, which, in turn, requires a general understanding of Native peoples just before contact. Teaching Period 9 is problematic because it comes at the end of the school year, and some classes might not cover the period as well as others. The weighting of content in the periods also has the benefit of guiding your teachers on how to focus on the common core of American history while allowing them to use historical materials that will be more interesting to you and thus be more effective in teaching historical thinking and reasoning skills. In studying how the Compromise of 1850 led to the Civil War, for example, students in California might focus on the controversies arising out of its admission to statehood while those in Massachusetts might spend more time studying the impact of the Fugitive Slave Law and the case of Anthony Burns.

APUSH also organizes U.S. history into eight themes to help you connect historical events and developments across time and to make possible deeper conceptual understanding of the big picture. Like periodization, organizing history around themes will help you to understand, explain, and analyze events. Themes connect events by crossing designated time periods and promote the kinds of questions that require the use of analytical reasoning: comparison, causation and consequences, and continuities and changes over time. What do historical developments have in common and/or do they contrast (Comparison)? Why did an event occur and/or what was its impact (Causation)? Does the event represent a continuation or break with the past (Continuity and Change over Time and Significance)?

APUSH Themes

Theme	Description
Theme 1: American and National Identity (NAT)	How and why of American and national identity
Theme 2: Work, Exchange, and Technology (WXT)	Factors behind the development of systems of economic exchange and the role of technology, markets, and government
Theme 3: Geography and the Environment (GEO)	The role of geography and both the natural and human-made environments on social and political developments
Theme 4: Migration and Settlement (MIG)	Why and how people moved to and within the United States
Theme 5: Politics and Power (PCE)	How different social and political groups influenced the society and government of the United States
Theme 6: America in the World (WOR)	The interactions between nations that affected North America and the influence of the United States on world affairs
Theme 7: American and Regional Culture (ARC)	How and why national, regional, and group cultures developed and changed
Theme 8: Social Structures (SOC)	How and why American systems of social organization developed and changed

As it is with periodization, discretion is involved in assigning events to themes. Because events and historical developments cannot be rigidly categorized, themes frequently overlap during analysis—for example, studying the internal migration of Americans can be thematically categorized in Migration and Settlement (MIG); Work, Exchange, and Technology (WXT); Geography and the Environment (GEO); Politics and Power (PCE); and American Regional Culture (ARC). How factual information is used depends on the focus in your studies. The cotton gin might appear in an essay on WXT (plantations changing from cultivating tobacco to cotton), MIG (stimulating the migration of slavery and plantation structures to the Black Belt), or PCE (affecting the influence of slave states in national politics). As with the mental rearrangement involved in periodization, seeing how an event fits into different themes helps you remember it, enhances your historical thinking and reasoning abilities, and provides you an opportunity to practice developing an historians' habit of mind.

A critical element of knowing history well is reflection and understanding, that is, thinking about historical events, individuals, and developments analytically. This means being able not only to **describe** what happened, where, by whom, and when, but to **explain** why, how, and "so what?" We find in our own studies that the instinctive or habitual search for the how, why, and "so what" actually helps us remember the what, when, by whom, and where. Reversing the process, knowing the how, why, and "so what" also helps us place new information into familiar thematic categories. Thinking analytically also means using questions associated with making connections (Contextualization) among events and determining causation and whether patterns changed over time. This process of looking for so many things in every fact sounds complicated, but in the end, such reflection leads to more effective learning. The key to this process is studying events and trying to learn as much as you can about their place in the big picture.

Using the Instructional Exam and Practice Exams

We wrote **AP U.S. History Prep** based on our collective experience teaching the APUSH course, writing questions as test developers, setting the criteria for scoring (grading), and reading the essays at the annual AP Reading. What follows is a practical guide for translating what you have learned in class into APUSH test-taking skills. Test construction and scoring (grading) is a complicated process that balances a number of variables designed to test whether the content and historical thinking skills on the exam are comparable to a college U.S. history survey. The test must ensure that the expected answers are accurate and, above all else, that every individual student gets the same, fair, and equal assessment on the written portions of the exam as each of the other 500,000 plus test takers. Before the exam is given to students, test designers chosen from college faculty and APUSH teachers review each question rigorously to ensure the answers (keys) are correct and that the content of the overall test is on subjects commonly taught in both APUSH and college classrooms. The essay portions of each exam, Free Response Section (FRQs)—the short-answer questions (SAQs), document-based question (DBQ), and long essay questions (LEQs)—are read and assessed (scored) at the annual APUSH Reading by about 2,000 readers, about 500 of whom read online. The Reading takes place around the first week in June.

Knowing how the FRQs are scored should help you present your learning so readers can see the strengths and quality of your responses. Keep in mind that over 500,000 students take APUSH; this means that there are potentially almost 3 million separate responses that must be read and scored within a short period of time. Making your thesis and argument explicit, your content historically accurate, and your writing clear will not only be beneficial to how you learn but will also allow readers to see and appreciate the merits of your responses. Each reader scores only one question; thus, each essay is scored by a different reader. To be scrupulously fair, APUSH wants each response to receive the same score that another of equal quality would receive—not only for the same question, but for every other question. For example, an essay with one score on an LEQ should get the same score as essays of similar quality on the other two LEQ choices. To facilitate consistency in the scoring process, a smaller group of readers known as Exam and Question Leaders pick sample essays in advance and determine the criteria readers must use as standards for measurement when they score the nearly three million responses.

With this in mind, we designed a process to help develop your knowledge of content and your historical thinking and reasoning skills and to improve your performance in the course and on the exam. In Chapters 3 and 4, we have provided an Instructional Exam and two Practice Exams. The Instructional Exam is intended to demonstrate how best to present your hard work and learning over the course of the school year; the two Practice Exams are provided to familiarize you with the exam format. The guidance given in the Instructional Exam is intended to develop the habits of mind that make taking the test much easier and less stressful. The 500 online multiple-choice questions (MCQs) provide you with additional practice and a further review of content.

Chapter 3 consists of the Instructional Exam, which has extensive suggestions for how to approach answering the MCQs and writing the FRQs. Along with sample questions, you will find detailed commentary designed to show you how to work through the MCQs and develop well-written, strong essays for the SAQs, DBQ, and LEQs that we believe will impress the readers. Chapter 4 consists of two Practice Exams, which are designed to be taken within exam time limits so that you become familiar with budgeting your time. We have also provided keys (answers) and suggestions for SAQ, DBQ, and LEQ responses for those Practice Exams.

We have broken down the Instructional Exam into a step-by-step walk-through of how to approach and to answer the MCQs and FRQs. The Instructional Exam in Chapter 3 contains two sets of MCQs, four SAQs, a DBQ, and three LEQs, each accompanied by detailed commentary about how to tackle each individual question. The two MCQ sets are intended to familiarize you with the question format and to explain why the answers (called keys) are correct and the other options (distractors) are incorrect. As Exam and Question Leaders, we have provided sample correct answers to the SAQs in a format that, in our experience, would receive points at the Annual Reading. For the MCQs and SAQs, you should read the introductory material to the question set, answer the question, check your answer (key), and then review the rationale (the explanation of why the key is correct).

On the exam, you will select three of the four SAQs. Three separate tasks are assigned to each SAQ; each task requires that you demonstrate your ability to connect factual information with a larger idea or theme. We suggest you do all four SAQs on the Instructional Exam to become familiar with the format and the content. One of the strengths of the SAQs is that a variety of specific factual information can be used to qualify for points. After you have responded to the separate prompts, spend some time trying to think of additional factual information that would qualify for points as part of your overall review.

The DBQ structure is a bit more involved, and you may choose to do one of two things:

1. **Write the DBQ as if you were taking the exam.**

   - Read the question.
   - Write your essay.

   ### Then

   - Compare your essay to the suggested thesis, document notes, suggested outlines, and commentary.
   - Make sure your use of evidence is historically accurate and defensible.
   - Reflect on the extent to which your essay follows the general historical thinking and reasoning processes we have outlined.
   - Review your essay and use the rubric to score it.
   - Re-read the documents, document notes, and commentary.
   - Reflect and think about changes you might make to strengthen your essay.

   ### Or

2. **Use the notes and sample outline and then write the DBQ.**

   - Read the question.
   - Read the documents one by one and review your understanding and analysis of them against the notes.
   - Develop a thesis or historically defensible claim.

- Arrange the documents in an outline.

- Write the essay.

Then

- Compare your essay to the suggested thesis, document notes, suggested outlines, and commentary.

- Make sure your use of evidence is historically accurate and defensible.

- Reflect on the extent to which your essay follows the general historical thinking and reasoning processes we have outlined.

- Review your essay and use the rubric to score your essay.

- Re-read the documents, document notes, and commentary.

- Reflect and think about changes you might make to strengthen your essay.

Every good historian revises and re-writes. Readers know that your essay is a first draft. Although you will not have the time to re-write your APUSH responses, reviewing your practice essay, re-reading the documents, and reflecting on them will act as (1) a review of the content of the period and theme and (2) a chance to work on the habits of writing good history. This is the functional equivalent of athletes practicing and reviewing films to observe their play and identify their mistakes.

You may find that your essay did not conform exactly to either of our two suggestions. This is to be expected. In any event, you should return to the second rubric we provide in the chapter and, in the space available, jot down the sentence or sentences in your essay that seem close to meeting the standard and would qualify for the point or points. For example, where the rubric asks for your thesis, state it. If you are unclear as to what your thesis was, think about how you might revise it and how your summary of the historical event is an explanation or argument that goes beyond just description. Think about how other events or developments might provide more background or context for the big picture. Consider what other evidence beyond the documents (outside information) you could include. Go back and re-read the documents and consider how you might have read them differently or how you might emphasize a different idea or phrase that would support your argument better. If you did not respond to the documents or the prompt in the ways that we suggest, this does not mean that your answer is incorrect, only that you may have had a different understanding than we did. This happens to historians all the time. Your concern should be whether your understanding is defensible by the facts—by language, ideas, or actions that you can find in the documents or from outside information. This is the moment for your honest reflection on what you wrote, how you read the documents, and whether you responded to the prompt with an historically defensible claim.

Chapter 3 has three LEQs because that is what the AP exam has. On the exam you will select only one on which to write. We suggest, however, that you do all three LEQs in the chapter. Write each separately, and after each compare it to our recommendations and advice to (1) practice with the format and structure, (2) reinforce the habits of asking why, how, and "so what?," and (3) review the content of the different historical periods. Your answers may differ from ours; you may use a slightly different thesis or argument or different facts to substantiate your position. Again, this is to be expected. As with the Instructional DBQ, the most important act is to reflect on your work and consider how you might revise or rethink what you have written to make it better, how you might alter or modify the thesis, how your analysis might shift in emphasis, what factual information you might add or substitute to support your thesis better, or whether the use of other facts might modify or qualify your argument.

Chapter 4 consists of two full-scale Practice Exams. We recommend that you take each exam under exam conditions within the allotted time limits and then consult the keys, document notes, and commentaries. As you review the MCQ keys, we recommend that you check any incorrect responses in your textbook or other references. The key is always the best answer, and the alternatives, called distractors for obvious reasons, sometimes contain partially correct information.

With the SAQs, a good way to review is to think about alternative responses that would qualify for the points. Again, this approach has the benefit of being more than just a plain review. The more specific, appropriate, historically accurate content you can provide in the SAQs, the more likely you are to be awarded the point. Finally, with the DBQs and LEQs, we again recommend that you practice while budgeting your time carefully. Be very disciplined and write under exam conditions so you become accustomed to the rhythms of taking the exam. We have all been in situations where we got excited and engaged in writing an essay on a topic about which we knew a great deal only to shortchange the other portions of our test. Getting two B essay answers is far better than getting an A and an F that results in receiving a C for the exam. You will have 1 hour and 40 minutes for the DBQ and LEQ; make sure you budget your time accordingly.

As with our recommendations for the Instructional Exam, go over the notes and commentary after you have written your essays and review your answers.

We stress this review process for two purposes. The primary, practical one is to help you develop the reasoning and argument skills critical to high scores on the DBQ and LEQs. The second is that when you review the content of your essays, you will benefit from both practicing the historians' habits of mind and from acquiring and retaining content knowledge. We are sure that you will see how useful the information and analyses are and how to apply the knowledge and content in other MCQs, SAQs, or LEQs that appear on your test.

Instructional Exam

We have designed this chapter to familiarize you with the different kinds of questions that appear on the AP exam and the ways in which they are scored or evaluated. We recommend that you approach the questions independently, answering the questions in each section and then reviewing the answers (keys) before moving on to the next section. For example, start with the Multiple-Choice Questions (MCQs) and review the answers. Then move on to the Short-Answer Questions (SAQs) and read our scoring notes; do the same with the Document-Based Questions (DBQs) and Long Essay Questions (LEQs). Please note that we designed the scoring notes for the SAQs, DBQs, and LEQs to match how we would put them together as guides for readers to use at the annual scoring of the writing portions of the exam.

Exam Overview

The exam is 3 hours and 15 minutes long and is broken down according to the table shown here.

Section	Question Type	Number of Questions	Exam Weight	Timing
I	Multiple-Choice Questions	55	40%	55 minutes
	Short Answer Questions (Students must answer 1 and 2, then choose either 3 or 4.)	3	20%	40 minutes
II	Document-Based Question	1	25%	60 minutes (includes suggested 15-minute reading period)
	Long Essay Question (Students select 1 of 3 choices.)	1	15%	40 minutes

Multiple-Choice Questions

Multiple-Choice Questions (MCQs) appear in sets of two, three, or four questions. Each set is preceded by a stimulus—a brief excerpt of text, a graph, or an image—followed by two, three, or four questions that are topically related to the stimulus. Each question is followed by four possible responses; the correct response is called the key, and the remaining three are distractors. Answering the question correctly requires an understanding of the stimulus and its context and point of view as well as content knowledge. Occasionally one question in a set is related topically but not specifically to the stimulus. It is a good idea to read all the answer choices because often distractors are partially correct; only the most accurate answer receives credit.

Tips for Answering MCQs

- Examine the source (author, date, and type) of the stimulus.

- Think about the historical context of the time period.

- Read or examine the stimulus carefully to understand the main idea.

- Read all answer choices.

- Eliminate answer choices that do not fit within the historical context.

- Select the option that best answers the question.

- Do not leave any answers blank. There is no penalty for guessing.

Source: *Pennsylvania Gazette*, 1754

1. Which of the following best represents the purpose of the above image?

    (A) It was intended to encourage the ratification of the Constitution.

    (B) It was created to support colonial demands for the right to settle west of the Appalachian Mountains.

    (C) It supported colonial cooperation during the French and Indian War.

    (D) It sought to discourage southern colonies from joining Spanish Louisiana and Florida.

Key: C

This image appeared in Benjamin Franklin's newspaper, *The Pennsylvania Gazette*, during the early years of the French and Indian War and reflects his support for the Albany Plan of Union, which was discussed at the Albany Congress in 1754.

- A is incorrect because the Constitutional Convention occurred in 1787.

- B is incorrect because the image does not address western settlement.

- D is incorrect because southern colonies did not wish to become part of Louisiana or Florida.

2. This image originally supported which of the following objectives?

   (A) Creation of a unified colonial government within the British Empire

   (B) Unity of the states during the War of 1812

   (C) Opposition of loyalists to independence

   (D) Recognition of New England as the leader of colonial protest

Key: A

Benjamin Franklin used the *Pennsylvania Gazette* to lobby for stronger colonial unity within the British system. Multiple facts can contribute to your knowing the key: the Albany Plan of Union, the Albany Congress, Franklin's role as colonial postmaster, his general support of royal government, and his publication of the *Gazette*. The key word in the stem is *"originally"*; knowing the context of the origins of the image is critical to identifying the key because the image was also used during the American Revolution.

- B is incorrect because it is outside the time period.

- C is incorrect because it is outside the time period.

- D is incorrect because New England is portrayed as the severed head of the snake.

3. How did the sentiments represented in this image change in the decades that followed?

   (A) Colonists ceased to produce cartoons like this one because they feared they might be accused of treason.

   (B) Cartoons like this one had little influence because newspapers had limited circulation.

   (C) These sentiments became more common as the colonies moved closer to actual rebellion.

   (D) Many felt that the southern colonies voiced widespread support for secession.

Key: C

The sentiments in this cartoon became much more popular as the momentum for revolution grew in the years following the French and Indian War. The image was recycled in 1765 with the protests over the Stamp Act; some representations substituted "Unite" for "Join."

- A is incorrect because open criticism of Great Britain became more frequent after 1766.

- B is false because colonial newspapers were highly influential.

- D is incorrect because secession was not a major issue among southern colonies in this time period.

CHAPTER THREE : INSTRUCTIONAL EXAM

"The Americans have been committed from the outset to the doctrine that all men are equal. We have elevated it to an absolute doctrine as a part of the theory of our social and political fabric. . . . It is an astonishing event that we have lived to see American arms carry this domestic dogma out where it must be tested in its application to uncivilized and half-civilized peoples. At the first touch of a test we throw the doctrine away and adopt the Spanish doctrine. We are told by all the imperialists that these people are not fit for liberty and self-government; that it is rebellion for them to resist our beneficence; that we must send fleets and armies to kill them if they do it; that we must devise a government for them and administer it ourselves; that we may buy them and sell them as we please, and dispose of their 'trade' for our own advantage. What is that but the policy of Spain to her dependencies? What can we expect as a consequence of it? Nothing but that it will bring us to where Spain is now."

> William Graham Sumner, "The Conquest of the United States by Spain,"
> speech given at Yale University before the Phi Beta Kappa Society in 1899.

1. Which of the following best explains the reasons for Sumner's speech?

   (A) The United States had begun to expand into the western Pacific.

   (B) The United States had begun to provide economic aid to Western Europe.

   (C) Sumner objected to the changes in diplomatic relations with China.

   (D) Theodore Roosevelt had just completed the modernization of the U.S. navy.

   Key: A

   This speech was given on the occasion of the American annexation of the Philippines after the Spanish-American War. Sumner was opposed to the expansion of the United States into the Philippines, especially after the Filipinos revolted against American rule.

   - B is incorrect because it is a reference to the Marshall Plan.

   - C is incorrect because it refers to the Open Door Policy.

   - D is incorrect because the stimulus emphasizes annexation rather than modernization of the American navy.

2. Sumner delivered this address as a result of which of the following U.S. actions?

   (A) The opening of vast areas of the western frontier to new immigrants

   (B) Establishment of the U.S. military as being the most powerful in the world

   (C) Acquisition of colonies after the Spanish-American War

   (D) Mediation of European disputes that threatened to lead to world war

   Key: C

   As a result of the Treaty of Paris of 1899, United States gained territory in the Pacific and needed to decide whether to grant those territories their independence or to annex them.

- A is incorrect because the frontier declared closed by the Census Bureau in 1890.

- B is incorrect because the U.S. military was not the most powerful at this time.

- C is incorrect because the United States did not mediate European disputes until later.

3. Which of the following groups would have agreed with Sumner's description of the conquered people?

(A) Supporters of the Social Gospel

(B) Proponents of Social Darwinism

(C) Transcendentalists

(D) Populists

Key: B

Social Darwinists believed that natural selection operated among men as it did in nature; therefore, some people were destined to rule and others, to be ruled. Sumner refers to those colonized, the Filipinos, as "uncivilized and half-civilized," and specifically refers to the necessity to suppress the rebellion for people who he thought were incapable of self-government. Sumner was a key proponent of Social Darwinism.

- A is incorrect because Sumner's description is inconsistent with the Social Gospel movement, which attempted to alleviate the poverty caused by urbanization.

- C is incorrect because the Transcendentalists were antebellum writers mostly centered in New England.

- D is incorrect because the Populists were part of a late-nineteenth-century political movement that was concerned about the rise of industrialization and urbanization.

CHAPTER THREE : INSTRUCTIONAL EXAM

Short-Answer Questions

The Short-Answer Questions (SAQs) account for 20% of the final AP exam score. Students have 40 minutes to respond to three SAQs. Questions 1 and 2 are mandatory, and then students must respond to either Question 3 or Question 4. Each SAQ has three parts designated A, B, and C; each part is worth 1 point, and students should answer all three parts for each SAQ.

Responses must be in complete sentences in order to receive credit. During the exam, a separate booklet is provided that students must use to answer their SAQs. Because responses to SAQs will be scanned for online scoring, answers to all three parts of each question should be no longer than one page. SAQ responses—all three parts together—are usually half to a full page in length (approximately 24 lines).

- Question 1 (mandatory) will include SECONDARY source stimuli. Parts A, B, and C will refer to the stimuli. This question will come from the time period 1754 to 1980 (Periods 3–8 in the Course Framework).

- Question 2 (mandatory) will include a PRIMARY source stimulus (frequently an image), and Parts A, B, and C will refer to that document. This question will also come from the 1754 to 1980 time period (Periods 3–8 in the Course Framework).

- Questions 3 and 4 will NOT have a stimulus, and you will choose one of the two. Question 3 will come from the periods 1491 to 1877 (Periods 1–5). Question 4 will come from the periods 1865 to 2001 (Periods 6–9). Both questions will have Parts A, B, and C, and you are expected to answer all three parts for the question you choose.

Writing the SAQ

Each SAQ most often begins with the phrase "Briefly explain" or "Briefly describe." Good responses will do exactly that—explain or describe briefly. Responses to SAQs do not require a thesis, and Parts A, B, and C do not require you to support a thesis, but responses must be in complete sentences. To get the point, responses may need more than one sentence to provide adequate explanation, description, or contextualization. Each Part is a separate question and is scored independently (1 point). There is no single format for responses. We recommend you write your responses separately: Part A—response; Part B—response; Part C—response. Some test takers choose to respond to all three Parts in a paragraph format. That is acceptable, but answers using this format are more difficult to score and may confuse readers. Again, all responses must be in complete sentences.

Those scoring the SAQs will decide if the response to each Part, A, B, C, is enough to get 1 point. You must clearly demonstrate accurate, appropriate historical knowledge in each part to receive the point. For example, if the question asks about the impact of technology on social life during the 1950s, the answer "People were moving to the suburbs" would not be enough to earn the point. The answer would require more specific information and context in order to receive the point. The answer would more likely get the point if it said "Because of the construction of the highway system, people could live in suburbs and commute to work in the cities." Or "Low-cost construction techniques led to suburban housing developments like Levittown." It is important that responses clearly show the context of the time period that is the subject of the question.

CHAPTER THREE : INSTRUCTIONAL EXAM

At their core, the SAQs ask you to demonstrate the historians' habits of mind, the processes of analysis and inquiry unique to the study of history, and your knowledge of the basic content of U.S. history to arrive at defensible answers. Each question tests the combination of your content knowledge and your ability to use historical thinking skills and reasoning processes. There is no single "correct" answer; rather, there are multiple possible correct answers because the SAQs are framed to allow for responses derived from the study of different specific events, individuals, or developments. While each question addresses specific AP "Historical Thinking Skills and Reasoning Processes" (Compare and Contrast, Cause and Effect, Continuity and Change) and "Themes," you may choose what historically defensible information you know that supports your argument.

Reminders for Writing SAQ Responses

- Each SAQ has three questions. Each question is worth **1** point. You must answer all three questions for three of the four SAQs on the AP test.

- Responses do NOT require a thesis, and Parts A, B, and C do not ask you to support a thesis statement.

- Separate the answers for each part: Part A—response; Part B—response; Part C—response.

- You may choose to answer all three parts in a single paragraph, but this format increases scoring difficulty.

- All responses must be in complete sentences.

The following sample SAQs replicate the order, format, and structure of SAQs as they appear on the exam. We include suggested possible responses after each sample question to demonstrate how sufficient, relevant content would score the point.

> **NOTE: Your answers to SAQs may vary depending on the content that you were taught in your classes. The exam has been designed to allow latitude in the specific content taught so there are multiple historically defensible answers. Where we have provided answers, they are suggestions only. Strong answers will demonstrate historically and contextually accurate statements that respond to the designated task.**

CHAPTER THREE : INSTRUCTIONAL EXAM

Short Answer Question 1 (Secondary Source Stimulus) Periods 3–8

"The makers of the federal Constitution represented the solid, conservative, commercial and financial interests of the county . . . [who] . . . drew together in a mighty effort to establish a government that would be strong enough to pay the national debt, regulate interstate and foreign commerce, provide for national defense . . . , and control the propensities of legislative majorities to attack private rights. . . . The radicals, however, like Patrick Henry, Jefferson, and Samuel Adams, were conspicuous by their absence from the convention. . . .

"[The makers of the Constitution were convened] to frame a government which would meet the practical issues that had arisen under the Articles of Confederation. The objections they entertained to direct popular government, and they were undoubtedly many, were based upon their experience with popular assemblies during the immediately preceding years.

". . . [T]hey naturally feared that the rights and privileges of the minority would be insecure if the principle of majority rule was definitely adopted and provisions made for its exercise. . . .

"They were anxious above everything else to safeguard the rights of private property against any leveling tendencies on the part of the propertyless masses."

Charles A. Beard, "Framing the Constitution," 1913.

"The Founding Fathers . . . were first and foremost superb democratic politicians.

"They were, with their colleagues, *political* men . . . and . . . were committed (perhaps willy-nilly) to working within the democratic framework, within a universe of public approval.

". . . [I]t was a *nationalist* reform caucus [convention] which had to operate with great delicacy and skill in a political cosmos full of enemies to achieve the one definitive goal—popular approbation [approval].

"What they did was to hammer out a pragmatic compromise which would both bolster the 'National interest' and be acceptable to the people."

John P. Roche, "The Founding Fathers: Reform Caucus in Action,"
American Political Science Association, December 1961

Using the excerpts above, answer (A), (B), and (C).

(A) Briefly describe ONE major difference between Beard's and Roche's historical interpretations of the framers of the United States Constitution.

(B) Briefly explain how ONE specific historical event or development during the period 1781 to 1787 could be used to support Beard's interpretation of the goals of the framers of the United States Constitution.

(C) Briefly explain how ONE specific historical event or development during the period 1776 to 1787 could be used to support Roche's interpretation of the goals of the framers of the United States Constitution.

Possible answers:

(A) To Beard, the framers of the U.S. Constitution (Founding Fathers) were wealthy conservative men who feared democracy or wanted a strong national government to protect their interests. Roche sees the framers as practical politicians who were willing to compromise to create a democratic government more responsive to the American people.

(B) Widespread, organized protests in Massachusetts, Virginia, and elsewhere led to fear of disorder and the need for stronger government. For example, the disorder of Shays's Rebellion led the framers identified by Beard to favor a strong government that would protect the interests of the propertied classes.

(C) The framers agreed to count three-fifths of the South's slave population for the purposes of representation in the House of Representatives.

Short Answer Question 2 (Primary Source Stimulus) Periods 3–8

"We, the representatives of the people of the Cherokee Nation, in Convention assembled, in order to establish justice, ensure tranquility, promote our common welfare, and secure to ourselves and our posterity the blessings of liberty . . . do ordain and establish this Constitution for the Government of the Cherokee Nation.

"**Article I.—Sec. 1:** The boundaries of this Nation, embracing the lands [beginning on the north bank of the Tennessee River] solemnly guarantied and reserved forever to the Cherokee Nation by the Treaties concluded with the United States . . . shall remain unalterably the same. . . .

"**Sec. 2:** The sovereignty and Jurisdiction of this Government shall extend over the country within the boundaries above described, and the lands therein are, and shall remain, the common property of the Nation."

> Constitution of the Cherokee Nation, July 1827

"**An act to add the Territory lying within the chartered limits of Georgia,** and now in the occupancy of the Cherokee Indians . . . and to extend the laws of this State over the same, and to annul all laws and ordinances made by the Cherokee nation of Indians. . . .

"**Sec. 6:** *And be it further enacted,* That all the laws both civil and criminal of this State be, and the same are hereby extended over said portions of territory respectively, and all persons whatever residing within the same, shall . . . be subject and liable to the operation of said laws."

> Laws of the Georgia State Assembly,
> December 19, 1829, and December 22, 1830

(A) Briefly explain the historical context of the two documents from the 1827–1830 period.

(B) Briefly explain ONE specific cause for the claims made by the legislature of the state of Georgia in the laws passed in 1829–1830.

(C) Briefly describe ONE specific outcome of the conflicting views expressed in the two documents.

Possible Answers:

(A) The two documents represent opposing positions for the removal of the Cherokee from Georgia.

(B) In exchange for surrendering its claims to western land, Georgia had received promises that Indian landholding would be eliminated, a position that Andrew Jackson made clear he supported.

(C) Jackson refused to recognize the Supreme Court's decision in *Worcester v. Georgia* that Georgia had no jurisdiction over the Cherokee Nation. This led to the expulsion of the Cherokee from Georgia in what became known as the Trail of Tears.

Students choose between Short Answer Questions 3 and 4.

Short Answer Question 3 (No Stimulus) Periods 1–5

(A) Briefly describe ONE specific example of religious diversity in the European colonies of North America settled before 1700.

(B) Briefly describe ONE specific example of religious diversity in the colonies established by settlers from Britain between 1607 and 1713.

(C) Briefly explain how religious enthusiasm in the British colonies in the 1740s led to religious diversity.

Possible Answers:

(A) The Spanish, French, and some English settlers brought Roman Catholicism to North America. Other English settlers brought the Church of England and Puritanism to the colonies. Unlike Europeans, Native American religious practices perceived a unified material and spiritual world where plants, animals, and humans shared divinity through a connection to guardian spirits.

(B) Lord Baltimore intended for the Maryland colony to be a haven for English Roman Catholics, and William Penn encouraged Quakers to settle in Pennsylvania. New England Puritans had to accommodate members of the Church of England in Massachusetts Bay while the Church of England was the established church in Virginia and South Carolina.

(C) The Great Awakening was an example of religious enthusiasm in the English colonies that encouraged the growth of evangelical denominations, such as Methodists and Baptists. Debates over religious enthusiasm also split congregations along lines of New Lights (enthusiasts) and Old Lights (legalists).

Short Answer Question 4 (No Stimulus) Periods 6–9

(A) Briefly describe ONE specific event that helped signal the end of the Cold War.

(B) Briefly explain ONE specific policy or action taken by the Reagan administration that helped bring about the end of the Cold War.

(C) Briefly explain ONE specific action taken by the United States that illustrated American foreign policy after the end of the Cold War.

Possible Answers:

(A) Increased military spending by the United States put pressure on the Soviet Union with which it could not keep up economically. The decline of the Soviet economy led to an economic collapse inside the U.S.S.R. Economic problems and revolutions against communist governments in Eastern Europe hastened the end of the Cold War. The fall of the Berlin Wall helped signal the end of the Cold War.

(B) The Reagan administration increased military pressure on the Soviet Union by enlarging the United States military. Negotiations with Gorbachev over economic and cultural exchanges and arms limitations put more pressure on the Soviet Union.

(C) The United States assumed the role of peacekeeper by intervening in the Middle East (Persian Gulf War), South and Central America (Nicaragua), and Eastern Europe (Bosnia) during the late 1980s and the 1990s.

The Document-Based Question

The Document-Based Question (DBQ) is unique to Advanced Placement history and constitutes 25% of your final score. It is a question or prompt that is to be answered using seven documents. The purpose of the DBQ is to determine your range of historical knowledge and how well you have mastered historical thinking and reasoning skills. Think about the prompt and documents as the raw materials for an essay. The prompt asks for a thesis or argument that uses the documents as evidence in the construction of the essay. You may worry that you do not know the subject of the DBQ in advance; however, you can do well if you have learned habits of mind, content, themes, and good essay writing skills. You need to understand that every document provides information and inferences that are relevant to answering the question. One key feature of every DBQ is that the use of evidence provided in the documents coupled with outside information can lead to high scores.

The APUSH rubric scores individual components of the essay separately: the thesis, contextualization, and the body (evidence, analysis and reasoning). Each component element is assigned a specific point value, and to obtain the points, the separate elements must demonstrate that they reach a specific level of achievement. Each point is earned independently. The rubric is designed to provide you with opportunities for partial credit and to ensure that readers distinguish and score the different elements of the essay.

DBQ Scoring Guidelines

Reporting Category	Scoring Criteria
Thesis (0–1 point)	**1 Point:** Responds to the prompt with a historically defensible claim that establishes a line of reasoning. May not simply restate or rephrase the prompt.
Contextualization (0–1 point)	**1 Point:** Describes a broader historical context relevant to the prompt.
Evidence (0–3 points) Evidence beyond the documents	**1 Point:** Uses the content of **three** documents to address the topic of the prompt (must accurately describe rather than quote). <div align="center">**or**</div>**2 Points:** Supports an **argument** in response to the prompt by accurately using at least **six** documents. <div align="center">**and**</div>**1 Point:** Uses at least one additional piece of specific evidence beyond that found in the documents relevant to the prompt.
Analysis and Reasoning (0–2 points)	**1 Point:** For at least **three** documents that explain how or why—rather than just identifying—the documents' point of view, purpose, historical situation, and/or audience is relevant to the argument.

	1 Point: Demonstrates a **complex understanding** of the historical development that is the focus of the prompt, using the evidence to corroborate, qualify, or modify an argument that addresses the question. This point may be satisfied in the following ways:
	    Qualifying or modifying a thesis or argument by considering historically defensible, diverse, or alternative perspectives of the evidence
	    Explaining both similarities and differences, continuity and change, multiple causation, or causes and consequences

If the rubric seems overly complicated, it is because it is designed to produce accurate scoring of exams, not to provide a guide to the writing of quality essays. The processes of learning to analyze historical events and documents and constructing a historical essay differ from the format of the scoring guide/rubric. That is to say, the scoring rubric works well in teaching you how to discover the strengths and weaknesses of your essay after you have written it. Write the DBQ first, then review it while asking yourself if you have satisfied the requirements of the different elements.

During your 15-minute reading period . . .

Approach writing the DBQ in the same way scholars do. Historians do not start by generating a thesis, describing a number of documents, and incorporating complex reasoning and arguments when they write. Instead, before historians begin, they have already read widely among the secondary literature, dived into primary sources, and, on the basis of their analysis, formed an answer to a question that addresses and illuminates a particular subject or theme. Too often students assume that they need to begin the process of writing a DBQ by immediately coming up with a thesis or opening argument rather than with the discovery and assessment of the evidence, an analysis of the available factual information, and the creation of generalizations that link the sources together. **Historians develop their theses (Section A of the Rubric) <u>after</u> they have examined and studied the evidence; so should you.** To develop a thesis (your answer to the question):

- As you read through each document, ask yourself how it helps answer the question.

- Identify relevant outside information that will also help answer the question.

- Examine the documents looking for ways to group them into categories that will help answer the questions.

- Identify documents that stand out because they can help you see unique points of view.

- Arrange your evidence in a way that helps you answer the question.

- Now develop your thesis, which takes a position and establishes categories that will help you answer all parts of the question.

Begin Your Essay

The Instructional DBQ asks you to answer the following:

Evaluate the extent to which the regulation of immigration during the period 1880 to 1924 was a response to economic and social factors.

In responding to the prompt, you should think about the Gilded Age, the Progressive Era, and the years after World War I. This period should be familiar to you as an era of rapid social and economic change during the late nineteenth–early twentieth centuries fueled by technological innovation, industrialization, and urbanization and accompanied by labor unrest, the rise of nativism, and the expansion of the federal government. This DBQ focuses on responses to the massive immigration that occurred during the period 1880 to 1924 and asks the extent to which the growth of regulatory policies of the federal government were an attempt to reduce economic and social dislocations. As with any DBQ, responses to this question will vary. Using the documents properly, there are no right or wrong answers, only better ones. **One requirement to consider is the necessity to use all or all but one of the documents.** Your thesis must present a historically defensible argument that fully addresses the question, uses the main idea of the documents to support your argument, and brings in outside information not included in the documents.

We suggest that your opening paragraph demonstrates how your thesis is set within a larger historical context. That means in presenting your thesis, your essay should show a connection between the impact of the Gilded Age on immigration during this period. Next complete your opening paragraph with your thesis statement, which answers the questions asked and establishes the categories of evidence you plan to discuss in your essay. This should earn you the contextualization point.

Do not start writing until you have understood the prompt, reflect on what is being asked, read the documents, and organize your thoughts.

Writing the DBQ

What follows is the Instructional DBQ and a guide to writing your essay. After you have completed your essay, read the **Suggestions for Writing the DBQ** section. We have provided a table of the DBQ rubric to use in helping you improve your essay. After you have completed your essay, use the table to identify where in your essay you satisfied the rubric to earn the point or points. We have also provided outlines of possible DBQ responses so you can see alternative ways of approaching this question. We will repeat the process with the two practice tests.

Evaluate the extent to which the regulation of immigration during the period 1880 to 1924 was a response to economic and social factors.

The following guides take the general instruction explained previously and apply them to this specific question.

Question Review and Thesis Formation: Read the question to determine what information you need to form a thesis.

- Establish the correct historical context for the question. **(Contextualization)**

- Write a thesis that directly answers all parts of the question, makes a historically defensible claim, and establishes the categories of analysis. **(Thesis)**

  - Identify key terms: "to what extent," "response," "economic and social instability."

  - Identify the central question being asked, the significance of the period 1880 to 1924, and what kinds of historical information both inside and outside the documents you need to answer the question.

- Consider events, facts, and historical developments that are relevant to the subject and can help provide a perspective that supports, modifies, or qualifies your thesis and argument.

- **Caution: Readers of the DBQ are instructed to grant the thesis point only if it is clearly identified in the first or last paragraph of the essay.**

Document Review: Read through the documents and take notes following the directions below. After you have completed your document review, check your research against our suggestions. Note that your observations may not be the same, but that does not mean your observations are wrong. Review the documents to verify your reading and analysis.

- Use all or all but one of the documents, explaining how they support your thesis.

- Determine how each document contributes to an explanation of the development of immigration regulations between 1880 and 1924. **(Evidence)**

- Introduce information not mentioned in the documents and explain how and why it relates to the documents and supports your thesis. **(Evidence beyond the Documents)**

- Arrange and organize the documents by common positions or points of view. Note that some documents will look favorably on immigrants, others unfavorably, and still others will be ambiguous. **(Evidence and Analysis and Reasoning)**

- **Sourcing:** Explain how and why the particular point of view, purpose, historical situation, and/or intended audience of at least three documents are significant to your argument.

- Create a safety net by sourcing more than three documents in case one of your three does not qualify for the point. **(Analysis and Reasoning)**

- Develop a tentative generalization or statement that includes all or all but one of the documents. Compare the claims or arguments in the documents and determine the extent to which they suggest a general but direct response to the prompt. **(Thesis and Evidence)**

- Determine the extent to which each document supports, challenges, or modifies your tentative generalization or thesis. **(Analysis and Reasoning)**

- Identify other facts, events, or historical phenomena that are related and support your modified thesis. **(Evidence beyond the Documents and Contextualization)**

Document 1

> Source: The Page Act 1875 (Sect. 141, 18 Stat. 477, 3 March 1875)
>
> "CHAP. 141. An act supplementary to the acts in relation to immigration.
>
> Be it enacted by the Senate and House of Representatives of the United States of America in Congress assembled, That in determining whether the immigration of any subject of China, Japan, or any Oriental country, to the United States, is free and voluntary, . . .
>
> SEC. 3: That the importation into the United States of women for the purposes of prostitution is hereby forbidden; and all contracts and agreements in relation thereto, made in advance or in pursuance of such illegal importation and purposes, are hereby dec1ared void; and whoever shall knowingly and willfully import, or cause any importation of, women into the United States for the purposes of prostitution, or shall knowingly or willfully hold, or attempt to hold, any woman to such purposes, in pursuance of such illegal importation and contract or agreement, shall be deemed guilty of a felony.
>
> * * *
>
> SEC. 5: That it shall be unlawful for aliens of the following classes to immigrate into the United States, namely, persons who are undergoing a sentence for conviction in their own country of felonious crimes other than political or growing out of or the result of such political offenses, or whose sentence has been remitted on condition of their emigration, and women 'imported for the purposes of prostitution.'"

Document 1

Main idea relevant to the question: The Page Act can be seen as an expansion of the national government into the regulation of morality and race. It bars the importation of Asian prostitutes and criminals.

Potential example of a statement of the main idea directly tied to the question: Concerns over increased criminal activity and prostitution on the West Coast led the U.S. government to impose restrictions on Asian immigrants entering the country.

Potential example of sourcing: Purpose: The Page Act was designed to alleviate fears and defuse social unrest among Americans who saw concentrations of Asian immigrants as a threat to American values and morality.

Possible Outside information: Chinese Exclusion Act, Chinese workers on railroads or as strikebreakers

Document 1 Notes

Document 1 should trigger a discussion on whether the regulation of immigration generally was designed to address the health, morals, or well-being of Americans or restrict the entry of aliens on the basis of race. Intended to address the importation of Asian, particularly Chinese, women, Document 1 (the Page Act) was a response to the large number of contract Chinese laborers entering the United States to work on the transcontinental railroads or to act as strikebreakers. The document should also remind students of the 1881 Chinese Exclusion Act, which also can be explained as an attempt to address either economic disorders in the labor market—that is, wage competition—or strike breakers. It can also be used to denote the racial restrictions on immigration by illustrating the fear of peoples who could not be Americanized. Alternatively, the regulation of prostitution represented a category of legislation related to the health, welfare, and benefit of Americans, such as Prohibition, national restrictions on lotteries, the Pure Food and Drug Act, and Child Labor. **(Contextualization and Evidence beyond the Documents)**

Document 2

Source: "Welcome to All!," *Puck*, April 28, 1880

WELCOME TO ALL!

WELCOME TO ALL!

Library of Congress, prints and photograph division, (LC-USZC4-954)

Document 2

Main idea relevant to the question: "Welcome to All!" illustrates that immigration was initially unrestricted and considered desirable. It should stimulate a discussion of immigration as a cause of the social and economic problems of the period.

Potential example of a statement of the main idea directly tied to the question: The United States originally saw itself as a place where European immigrants, displaced by social and economic unrest, could find refuge and contribute to the economic growth of the country.

Potential example of sourcing: Historical Situation: European immigrants, pushed by social and economic unrest and pulled by the tremendous economic growth associated with the Second American Industrial Revolution, were welcomed by the United States as a cheap source of labor.

Possible outside information: Industrial Revolution; congestion in the cities; sweatshops; Lincoln Steffens, *Shame of the Cities*; Jacob Riis, *How the Other Half Lives*; Statue of Liberty ("Give me your tired . . ."); Hull House; dumbbell tenements

Document 2 Notes

Document 2 ("Welcome to All!") expresses the demand for labor and promotes the idea of America as a refuge for the world (the sign above the door and the sign before the ramp) that attracted large numbers of immigrants.

Document 3

> Source: John Miller (R-Calif.), Speech to the Senate, February 28, 1881
>
> Cheap labor is not a cause of any public good, but an effect of a vicious economic system. It is necessary to a perception of the truth, in the investigation of such questions, to consider the principles of that higher political economy which not only elucidates the laws which govern production and distribution of wealth but subjects the elements and causes of national prosperity or adversity to searching philosophical analysis. . . . Temporarily, and under peculiar conditions, cheap labor might be an advantage, but when we consider our condition and are confronted by the fact that the introduction of an alien race of men who perform the cheap labor operates as a displacement of the natives of the soil, man for man and substitutes a non-assimilative, heterogeneous people utterly unfit for and incapable of free or self-government, the question assumes proportions which are not to be reassured by the application of mere economic theories.

Document 3

Main idea relevant to the question: John Miller's speech to the Senate, using social science to address social problems and relying on race as a criterion for acceptability. Justifies legislation restricting immigration on the grounds that it undermines American prosperity and capacity for self-government.

Potential example of a statement of the main idea directly tied to the question: Many in the United States continued to harbor nativist views that immigrants represented an inferior class of people and threatened the economic livelihood of American workers.

Potential example of sourcing: Point of View: Miller's nativist and racist views were important because they galvanized support for immigration regulation by implying that the lack of immigration restriction would lead to economic and social unrest in the United States.

Possible outside information: Chinese Exclusion Act; Molly Maguires; North Adams, Massachusetts, strikebreakers; American Protective Association; Immigration Restriction League

Document 3 Notes

While Document 3 does not refer specifically to the Chinese, it asserts that the importation of immigrants causes low wages that hurt native-born workers. (Knowledge of the episodes of the participation of immigrant strikebreakers at North Adams, Massachusetts, or the Molly Maguires (who were Irish) would be, like Chinese exclusion, useful additional Evidence beyond the Documents. The document also refers to the problem of assimilating immigrants.

Document 4

Source: U.S. inspectors examining eyes of immigrants, Ellis Island, New York Harbor, New York. © Underwood & Underwood, c. 1913.

11164-U. S. Inspectors examining eyes of immigrants, Ellis Island, New York Harbor. Copyright Underwood & Underwood, U-97332

Library of Congress, Print and Photographs Division (LC-USZ62-7386)

Document 4

Main idea relevant to the question: Immigrants had to undergo physical examinations before being allowed to enter the U.S. This rule, which expanded the sphere of federal regulations, was intended to ensure that immigrants did not bring diseases into the country.

Potential example of a statement of the main idea directly tied to the question: American fears that disease carried by immigrants would lead to epidemic outbreaks in the United States spurred the federal government to require physical examinations before immigrants could enter the country.

Potential example of sourcing: Historical Situation: The entry of increasing numbers of poverty-stricken Southern and Eastern European immigrants, coupled with racist stereotypes, resulted in the American people pressuring the federal government to enact legislation ensuring the good health of those who entered the country.

Possible outside information: Use of physical examinations to disqualify immigrants from entering, Statue of Liberty, anarchy, socialism, literacy tests

Document 4 Notes

Document 4 is intended to stimulate a discussion of the health of immigrants as a criterion for entry into the United States. The physical examination of immigrants represented official barriers imposed primarily against immigrants from Southern and Eastern Europe. That these documents contradict each other speaks to the complex nature of the disputes and the importance of understanding the point of view of the authors, the function of the documents, and the problem of social science methodologies. This document could also be used more explicitly than the other documents to demonstrate both the reluctance to admit the new immigrants and/or the rise of Progressive Era legislation that called for the expansion of the role of government to bring stability to American social and political life.

Document 5

Source: Max J. Kohler, "Some Aspects of the Immigration Problem," *American Economic Review* 4:1 (March 1914): 93–108

"Disinterested social workers who have devoted their lives to studying these new immigrants find that they are being rapidly absorbed, and are valuable increments to our population. . . .

* * *

Nor should we forget that it is the illiterate immigrant, victim of inferior conditions in his own country, upon whom we depend to do work which the more literate laborer will not perform— working our farms, digging our subways, excavating our lots, and operating our mines. . . .

* * *

Mr. Bryce also suggests that nearly all "the instreaming races are equal in intelligence to the present inhabitants"; that a blending of races tends to stimulate intellectual fertility; and that the Jews, Poles, and Italians are likely to "carry the creative power of the country to a higher level of production" than it has yet reached. He also notes that "today, most of the hard, rough toil of the country is everywhere done by recent inhabitants from central or southern Europe. The Irish and the urban part of the German population have risen in the scale, and no longer form the bottom stratum."

Document 5

Main idea relevant to the question: Kohler argues that new immigrants are a benefit to the United States and that America needs cheap labor for unskilled jobs. Research studies, according to Document 5, illustrate that new immigrants will be upwardly mobile in the future.

Potential example of a statement of the main idea directly tied to the question: Many Americans believed that hardworking immigrants from Southern and Eastern Europe who assumed low-paying jobs showed the same capacity for assimilation into American economic and intellectual society as did Irish and German immigrants from an earlier era.

Potential example of sourcing: Purpose or Historical Situation: Kolher was attempting to disarm immigration restriction advocates by citing the advances made by previous generations of immigrants who entered the country with similar liabilities. Much of this effort would be undone during World War I by propaganda efforts against nationalities associated with the Central Powers.

Possible outside information: *Muller v. Oregon,* Committee on Public Information, Creel Committee, literacy tests

Document 5 Notes

Document 5 argues that new immigrants improve the economic and social health of the United States. The text is from a social science study that was a common inspiration for Progressive legislation. A second reading illustrates how it still uses race to categorize workers but argues for a ladder migration theory: As new immigrants come in, they take the low-paying jobs of previous immigrants, who then move up in social and economic status.

Document 6

Source: Harry H. Laughlin, Testimony before U.S. House Committee on Immigration Committee, *Hearings,* April 17, 1920

"The character of a nation is determined primarily by its racial qualities; that is, by the hereditary physical, mental and moral or temperamental traits of its people. . . .

* * *

[A]s in the case of the insane, the feeble-minded and practically all other types of the socially inadequate are recruited more numerously from recent immigrant stock, in proportion to its total number, than from our older settlers. Apparently, the quality of our immigration is declining. It is not so much a matter of nationality—that is, northern European blood against southern European blood—as of skimmed milk versus cream in each of the countries sending us immigrants. In reference to foreigners, one notices, by the names of individuals who are found in institutions, that the lower or less progressive races furnish more than their quota. . . .

* * *

It is doubtful whether there is a single country in the world that does not have many families so splendidly endowed by nature that they would not make excellent and desirable additions to our citizenry. But because our foundation stock is largely from northwestern Europe and our national life was largely determined after the northwestern Europe pattern, we find the assimilation of immigrants from this section of Europe to be a much simpler task than the Americanization of Latin or other stocks less closely related to us in nationality. We like to think also that the percentage of hereditary excellence is higher in our parental countries of Europe than in other nations. Perhaps it is; but by setting up an eugenical standard for admission demanding a high natural excellence of all immigrants regardless of nationality and past opportunities, we can enhance and improve the national stamina and ability of future Americans. At present, not inferior nationalities but inferior individual family stocks are tending to deteriorate our national characteristics. Our failure to sort immigrants on the basis of natural worth is a very serious national menace."

Document 6

Main idea relevant to the question: In the debates over immigrant restriction, Harry Laughlin argues the new immigrants from Southern and Eastern Europe are incompatible with earlier immigrants from Northern Europe and are undermining American culture and institutions.

Potential example of a statement of the main idea directly tied to the question: During the economic, social, and political unrest that followed World War I, there was a return to nativist and racist views of the late nineteenth century and the fear that the innate inferiority of Southern and Eastern European immigrants would undermine the cultural purity of the American people.

Potential example of sourcing: Historical Situation: The negative stereotyping of certain nationalities during World War I, and the Red Scare that followed, led many Americans to call for discriminatory immigration legislation against nationalities that were considered substandard.

Possible outside information: Madison Grant, Immigration Restriction League, American Protective Association, literacy test, Committee on Public Information, Red Scare, anarchy, socialism, Emma Goldman, Soviet Ark, Palmer Raids

Document 6 Notes

Document 6 can be used as evidence for scientific reasons that support regulating the ethnic population of the United States. First, Laughlin is testifying before a congressional committee on immigration. Laughlin asserts the creation of the United States is mostly settled by Northern European immigrants who make up "a high percentage of hereditary excellence." He further argues that "inferior family stocks are tending to deteriorate our national characteristics." The argument also rests on claims to scientific validity used in support of determining the social health of the nation.

Document 7

Source: Le Baron Colt (R, RI), Speech to the Senate, April 2, 1924

"There are some people who believe in total suspension of immigration. There are others who believe in restriction to the lowest number, . . . independent of economic or humanitarian considerations. . . . [T]here are those who want to carry the quota basis back to 1890. . . .

* * *

. . . If you go back to 1890, you have 87 per cent from northern and western Europe and 13 per cent from southern and eastern Europe. Do you wonder that the 6,000,000 people [immigrants] from southern and eastern Europe claim that this is a gross discrimination against them? . . . I have set my foot down against, not for the reason that there are people over in southern and eastern Europe who want to come here, oh, no; but for the reason that we have more than 6,000,000 of these people here whom we want to make good American citizens.

Is this country going to adopt the non-American policy of classifying 6,000,000 of our foreign born as undesirables? Are we for the first time in our history, going to raise so far as Europe and the white race is concerned, this question of racial antagonism and racial prejudice, which has wrecked more than half of Europe?

. . . Raise that question that they are undesirable and you sow the seed of discontent and bitterness, not only among the 6,000,000 but among the 18,000,000 if we include the children of these 6,000,000 for they feel this discrimination just as keenly."

Document 7

Main idea relevant to the question: Colt argues that Southern and Eastern European immigrants should not be considered undesirables and that restricting their entry is discriminatory and would cause discontent.

Potential example of a statement of the main idea directly tied to the question: During the economic, social, and political unrest that followed World War I, there was a return to nativist and racist views of the late nineteenth century and the fear that the innate inferiority of Southern and Eastern European immigrants would undermine the cultural purity of the American people.

Potential example of sourcing: Historical Situation: The negative stereotyping of certain nationalities during World War I, and the Red Scare that followed, led many Americans to call for discriminatory immigration legislation against nationalities that were considered substandard.

Possible Outside Information: Red Scare, quota systems, National Origins Act, Emergency Quota Act of 1921, Sacco and Vanzetti

Document 7 Notes

Document 7 occurred during the debate over the National Origins, or Johnson–Reed, Act of 1924, which established limits on immigration by national origin. Colt considers Southern and Eastern Europeans as white. If Southern and Eastern Europeans are white, then they should be allowed to immigrate while Asians or Africans should not. Documents 5 and 6 still imply that Southern and Eastern Europeans are distinctive ethnic or racial groups even if holding different points of view as to their ability to contribute to American life. Colt also uses social science arguments typical of the Progressive Era to rebut ideas like those of McLaughlin and Grant.

Possible examples to earn the complexity of understanding point for the overall essay:

- In order to earn the complexity point, your essay might examine the ways in which the regulation of immigration was a response to political factors.

- In order to earn the complexity point, your essay might examine the degree to which calls for immigration restriction in earlier periods (1840s and 1850s) were a response to social and economic factors.

Question Review and Thesis Formation

- **Caution: DBQ Readers are instructed to grant the thesis point only if it is clearly identified in the first or last paragraph of the essay.**

- Establish the correct historical context in which the question is based. **(Contextualization)**

- Write a thesis that directly answers all parts of the question, makes a historically defensible claim, and establishes the categories of analysis **(Thesis)**.

  - Identify key terms: "to what extent," "response," "economic and social instability."

  - Identify the central question being asked, the significance of the period 1880 to 1924, and what kinds of historical information both inside and outside the documents are needed to answer the question.

- Consider events, facts, and historical developments that are relevant to the subject and can help provide a perspective that supports, modifies, or qualifies your thesis and argument. **(Analysis and Reasoning)**

Document Review: First read the documents and

- Use all or all but one of the documents, explaining how they support your thesis.

- Determine how each document contributes to an explanation of the development of immigration regulations between 1880 and 1924. **(Evidence)**

- Introduce information not mentioned in the documents and explain how and why it relates to the documents and supports your thesis. **(Evidence beyond the Documents)**

- Arrange and organize the documents by common positions or points of view. Note that some documents will look favorably on immigrants, others unfavorably, and still others will be ambiguous. **(Evidence and Analysis and Reasoning)**

- Identify the source and date, the particular point of view, purpose, historical situation, and/or intended audience of at least three documents and determine how that might be significant to your argument. Create a safety net by doing this for more than three documents in case one of your three does not qualify for the point. **(Analysis and Reasoning)**

- Develop a tentative generalization or statement that includes all or all but one of the documents. Compare the claims or arguments in the documents and determine the extent to which they suggest a general but direct response to the prompt. **(Thesis and Evidence)**

- Determine the extent to which each document supports, challenges, or modifies your tentative generalization or thesis. **(Analysis and Reasoning)**

- Identify other facts, events, or historical phenomena that are related and support your modified thesis. **(Evidence beyond the Documents and Contextualization).**

Suggestions for Writing the DBQ on Immigration, 1880–1924

This DBQ asks you to reflect on the way in which the regulation of immigration during the period 1880 to 1924 illustrates a response to the dramatic social, cultural, and economic changes that accompanied industrialization and urbanization. The coincidence of the arrival of the new immigrants and the problems of the cities—poverty, congestion, rising death rates, and labor unrest—suggested to observers that if immigrants were the cause of these problems, regulating their entry provided a possible solution.

Likely approaches to the DBQ also illustrate how the prompt can lead to different responses while still using the same body of documents. Our suggestions rest on the assumption that issues surrounding immigration in the period 1880 to 1924 reflect multiple historical developments. The period preceding 1880 was marked by technological innovation and the rise of industrial capitalism. Accompanying these changes was a surge of immigration that differed from previous patterns. Whereas previous immigrants from Europe had been from the British Isles and Western Europe, a large proportion of the new immigrants came from Southern and Eastern Europe and were Catholic or Jewish. In the search for solutions to the dislocations caused by industrialization and urbanization, the regulation of immigrants in the period illustrates

- growing involvement of the federal government in insuring the morality, health, and well-being of Americans,

- the emergence of nativism or anxiety over the potential loss of traditional American institutions and culture,

- the way in which Progressive reforms rested the emerging use of social science as a response to social problems.

In our sample responses, we have noted the way in which sample essay 3 is integrated into the guides to responses for alternatives 1 and 2. Crucial to the development of a strong essay is how the thesis is presented and content of the documents used to support its argument. Outlines of two possible essays follow.

Essay Outline 1

Thesis and Contextualization

The regulation of immigration was the attempt by the federal government to respond to the social and economic problems of the Gilded Age through the years following World War I. As the Industrial Revolution led to problems associated with urbanization, poverty, and labor strife, American attitudes toward immigrants began to change. Government regulations on immigration, particularly that from Southern and Eastern Europe, were seen as a way to improve the health and welfare of Americans.

Evidence, Analysis, and Reasoning

Social and Economic

> **Document 2 ("Welcome for All!")** stimulates a discussion of how policies regarding immigration in the period 1880 to 1924 reflected attempts to adjust to social and economic changes that began before 1880. As immigrants arrived to take up work in factories, the cities became crowded and unhealthy.

> **Document 1** (the Page Act) prohibits the entry of Asian prostitutes. An inference of its purpose is that it is intended to protect the moral health of citizens of the United States.

Regulation and Arguments

Documents 1 and 3 (speech by John Miller) illustrate arguments in favor of the regulation of immigration to insure the health and prosperity of the United States. Document 1 addresses morality, and Document 3 attacks immigration on the grounds that it produces low wages. Document 3 implies that immigration caused poverty and poor conditions in the city.

Document 4 (Ellis Island) represents the regulations enacted to ensure that immigrants were healthy. Immigrants who did not satisfy the requirements were returned to their countries of origin.

Documents 5 (Kohler), 6 (Laughlin), and 7 (Colt) illustrate the contested nature of immigration restrictions. Documents 5 and 7 are opposed to restrictions on Southern and Eastern European immigrants, arguing that they are not the cause of poor conditions in the United States, and Document 6 supports such restrictions to protect American society. Although Document 7 favors not restricting immigration for Southern and Eastern Europeans, the author does so by including these immigrants among the white race.

Dramatic increases in the number of immigrants and the diversity of their origins (Southern and Eastern Europe) created challenges to American society and economy. These restrictions were a response to the increase in immigrants and were as seen as means to address these challenges. From this perspective, previous unrestricted immigration had led to overcrowded cities filled with migrants who were thought to be responsible for rising levels of urban poverty, low wages, and the appearance of cultures inconsistent with American values. A response using this approach should focus on the attributes in the documents that addressed the health and moral benefits that would be gained through the regulation of immigration. Documents 1 (the Page Act) and 4 (Ellis Island) are highly useful in this regard. In Document 1, you would focus on the regulation of morals (the prohibition against prostitution), and Document 4 simply documents the idea that immigrants should not have eye diseases before entering the United States. The remaining documents can then be addressed in terms of how immigration restrictions promoted the health, welfare, and benefit of Americans particularly in economic terms (wages) or in terms of cultural assimilation.

Note that all the documents illustrate a central characteristic of Progressive reform in that they use supposedly social science methods and evidence in support of the regulations. The eye exam portrayed in the Ellis Island image illustrates government making sure that immigrants entering the United States are healthy and would not be burdens on other Americans; the physical exams are similar to regulations governing women's working hours and child labor (see *Muller v. Oregon*, Child Labor Act—**Evidence beyond the Documents, Contextualization**) that provide links to larger thematic developments.

Essay Outline 2

Thesis and Contextualization

The growth of immigrant regulation was the product of growing nativism resting on the belief that the immigrants could not be assimilated culturally. Industrialization and urbanization in the second half of the nineteenth century created large cities marked by poverty, labor strife, and many communities of first-generation immigrants. Confusing the economic and social instability of the Gilded Age with the arrival of many new immigrants from Southern and Eastern Europe, native-born Americans feared that the immigrants threatened traditional cultural and political institutions and began to impose regulations restricting the numbers of immigrants who would be allowed to enter the United States.

Evidence and Analysis and Reasoning

Social and Economic

> **Document 2 ("Welcome for All!")** stimulates a discussion of how industrialization led to welcoming immigrants to fill the demand for labor in the United States, but at the same time the new immigrants from Southern and Eastern Europe seemed to be responsible for the problems of the crowded cities, labor strife, and urban poverty.

> **Document 4 (Ellis Island)** illustrates the increased regulation imposed on the new immigrants. The document should lead to a statement regarding the growth of regulations on immigrants in the period 1880 to 1924.

Nativism

> **Documents 1 (the Page Act), 3 (James Miller), and 6 (Harry Laughlin)** use the race or ethnic origin as a criterion to advocate for the restriction of immigrants. Document 1 prohibits Asian women generally but it, like Document 3, should lead to a discussion of the Chinese Exclusion Act. Document 6 notes the benefits of Northern European immigrants while arguing that Southern Europeans are diluting the excellence of American institutions.

> **Document 4 (Ellis Island)** is an example of the growth of regulations in response to the new immigration. The document also represents other regulations that weighed more heavily on immigrants from Southern and Eastern Europe.

> **Documents 5 (Kohler) and 7 (Colt)** challenge the restrictions but still retain the nativist categories in their defense of Southern and Eastern European immigrants. Document 5 notes the contributions that unskilled laborers make to the economy and states that their integration into American society will be a benefit. Document 7 argues that the proposed restrictions on immigrants discriminates against some whites and sows discontent. It also implies that Colt supports the immigrants because they may be part of his political constituency.

The second suggested response requires you draw out of the documents the elements that demonstrate how regulations became increasingly more restrictive in racial terms. Your essay would discuss how immigration regulations gradually increased until they limited the entry of Southern and Eastern Europeans and prohibited Asians in the National Origins Act (1924). Document 4 (Ellis Island) is one of those ambiguous documents that can lead you to write a stronger, more complex essay. Although the image seems to be a simple regulation, eye exams, the addition of physical exams created additional requirements that immigrants needed to satisfy. If immigrants failed their physicals, they were sent back to their countries of origin. The documents also encourage you to have a more complicated thesis in that the acknowledgment and use of race as criteria for regulation did not necessarily mean hostility to the new groups. A good essay would also document changes in attitude toward the new immigrants from hostility to one of welcoming of their new ideas as a positive influence on the American economy, political system, and society.

We have provided a table with the rubric. After writing your DBQ essay, use the table to determine if you have satisfied the scoring points. Use the space within the table to identify the part of your essay that you think will satisfy the points.

DBQ Scoring Guidelines

Reporting Category	Scoring Criteria
Thesis (0–1 point) My Thesis	**1 Point:** Responds to the prompt with a historically defensible claim that establishes a line of reasoning. May not simply restate or rephrase the prompt.
Contextualization (0–1 point) Identify Contextualization	**1 Point:** Describes a broader historical context relevant to the prompt
Evidence (0–4 points) Note: You either get 1 or 2 points depending on how many documents you use accurately. List Evidence from the documents Outside Information	**1 Point:** Uses the content of **three** documents to address the topic of the prompt (must accurately describe rather than quote) **or** **2 Points:** Supports an **argument** in response to the prompt by accurately using at least **six** documents. **and** **1 Point:** Uses at least one additional piece of specific evidence beyond that found in the documents relevant to the prompt.

Analysis and Reasoning (0–2 points)
 	
Identify Sourcing
 	
Identify Complex Understanding
	1 Point: For at least **three** documents that explain how or why—rather than just identifying—the documents' point of view, purpose, historical situation, and/or audience is relevant to the argument.
	
	1 Point: Demonstrates a complex understanding of the historical development that is the focus of the prompt, using the evidence to corroborate, qualify, or modify an argument that addresses the question. This point may be satisfied in the following ways:
	
	    Qualifying or modifying a thesis or argument by considering historically defensible, diverse or alternative perspectives of the evidence
	    Explaining both similarities and differences, continuity and change, multiple causation, or causes and consequences

Long Essay Questions

Long Essay Questions (LEQs) are similar to the kinds of essays you will find in college courses and share some common elements with the DBQ. You will select one of three choices and have 40 minutes to write your essay. It is worth 15% of your score. Designed to assess how well you have learned the basic content and themes of U.S. history, LEQs require you to present your knowledge in the form of an argumentative, historically defensible essay. Unlike the DBQ, LEQs do not test your ability to read and analyze documents; they assess your ability to use your own knowledge of content to explain a major historical event, development, or theme. Like the DBQ, LEQs ask you to assert a thesis or historically defensible claim, demonstrate the ability to contextualize your discussion, and supply evidence to support it. Although the LEQs demand knowledge of more specific content knowledge than the DBQ, you still have some discretion over the evidence you supply to substantiate your thesis or argument.

Writing a response to an LEQ differs from responding to the DBQ because you must supply your own evidence. If you have worked hard at developing a historians' habits of mind, you should choose the question on the period that you understand best. While knowing more is better than knowing less, success on LEQs depends on the combination of factual knowledge and understanding its relationships. To accomplish this requires using comparisons of events and historical developments and examining causation or continuity or change over time. Having selected wisely, you will be better prepared to know how to set out a logical chain of reasoning that responds to the prompt (Thesis) and to select the factual information that will best help you score points on contextualization, evidence, and analysis and reasoning. As with the DBQ, we have developed a step-by-step guide to writing LEQs. Review the rubric in the table, review the three LEQs, then follow the instructions and write your response to each LEQ.

Although you will have to respond to only one LEQ on the APUSH exam, doing all three will have two very important advantages. First, it will give you additional experience within writing long essays. Just as scholars improve their writing with practice, you too will benefit from practice. Second, the act of writing the three essays will help you review the subject and time period, which will reinforce your content knowledge. We recommend that you first select a question, note how we have set up outlines for answers, then use the outline to write your answer. After you have completed your essay answer, use the rubric to determine whether you have satisfied the criteria for scoring the point or points. Then, depending on how well you think you did, write the next essay without referring to the suggested outline. Then use the outline to check your work against the rubric.

Note the following: The DBQ is numbered 1 on the exam while the LEQs are numbered 2 to 4. All LEQs test one of the following skills: causation, comparison, or continuity and change over time.

Long Essay Rubric

Reporting Category	Scoring Criteria
Thesis/Claim (0–1 point)	**1 Point:** Responds to the prompt with a historically defensible claim that establishes a line of reasoning.
Contextualization (0–1 point)	**1 Point:** Describes a broader historical context relevant to the prompt.
Evidence (0–2 points)	**1 Point:** Provides specific examples of evidence relevant to the prompt. **or** **2 Points:** Supports an argument using specific and relevant examples of evidence.
Analysis and Reasoning (0–2 points)	**1 Point: Uses historical reasoning (comparison, causation, continuity and change.** **or** **2 Points:** Demonstrates a **complex understanding** of the historical development that is relevant to the prompt using evidence to corroborate, qualify, or modify an argument that addresses the question.

Please remember that you have a total time of 1 hour and 40 minutes for writing the Free Response Questions (DBQ and LEQ). We suggest that you spend 60 minutes on the DBQ and use the remaining 40 minutes to write the LEQ. Budget your time! The proctor will announce the suggested time for each section, but you are responsible for managing your own progress.

Writing the LEQ

- Read all three questions and select the one you feel best prepared to answer.

- Establish the correct historical context for the question.

- Write a thesis that directly answers all parts of the question, makes a historically defensible claim, and establishes the categories of analysis. **(Thesis)**

  - Identify key terms.

  - Identify the central question being asked, the significance of the period, and what kind of historical information is needed to answer the question.

  - Assemble a brief list of facts relevant to the question.

- Reflect and consider how your facts support an argument or interpretation that responds to the prompt.

- Select the facts that best illustrate and explain how they provide an argument or interpretation that responds to the prompt.

- **Caution: You must provide the thesis statement in the first or last paragraph of the essay.**

2. **Evaluate the impact of British policy after the Seven Years' War (French and Indian War) on colonial politics in the period 1763 to 1776.**

Thesis and Contextualization

Britain's efforts to reform its organization of North America after the Seven Years' War and to make its enlarged empire more financially viable through new taxes and regulations led to the rise of colonial protest and discontent and ultimately independence. Previous absence of strict enforcement of trade regulations and the development of colonial self-government led to greater discontent with Britain's new policies after the war.

Evidence and Analysis and Reasoning

The following may be included but you are not limited to

- Political reactions to the Stamp Act, such as the colonial assemblies' resolutions, mass protests, Stamp Act Congress, Benjamin Franklin's lobbying efforts in Parliament

- Petitions to Parliament from colonial assemblies

- Resistance to taxes on commodities, primarily tea, which included boycotts and nonimportation agreements

- Increasing resistance and hostility to British policies and actions as exhibited by the reaction to the Boston Massacre.

- Organized defiance to British laws: the Boston Tea Party

- Coercive/Intolerable Acts leading to the Continental Congress

Complexity Point

- Asserting colonists willingness to pay external rather than internal or regulatory rather than revenue taxes

- Recognizing the British need to raise revenues to help defend the colonies

- Colonial leaders using Enlightenment philosophy to justify their positions

3. **Evaluate the impact of the Civil War on the U.S. economy in the period 1865 to 1900.**

Thesis and Contextualization

In response to the Southern states seceding in 1860–1861, Lincoln called out the U.S. army. In order to end the rebellion, Lincoln and others realized the necessity of expanding the military and finding ways to equip it and to commit economic institutions to new, better, and quicker ways to produce and manufacture goods for the war effort. The war stimulated the growth of railroads; of coal, steel, and textile production; and of business organization and techniques designed to increase manufacturing efficiency and speed. Many manufacturers and businessmen accumulated vast amounts of capital that they used in the post–Civil War decades to expand the nation's economy and wealth.

Evidence and Analysis and Reasoning

The following may be included but you are not limited to

- Growth of railroads for more rapid movement of troops and supplies, for reducing costs and time of shipping, and for stimulating greater production in key industries, such as coal, timber, and steel

- Pacific Railroad Act of 1862 providing government subsidies to encourage construction of the transcontinental railroad, which facilitated the settlement of the Great Plains and encouraged the hiring of immigrant labor (Chinese and Irish)

- Homestead Act of 1862 making land more available for settlers and increased farming of the Great Plains (McCormick reaper, steel plows, crops, and mineral production) that in turn lowered food prices and helped improve the standard of living

- National Banking Act of 1863 organizing banking and the nation's currency

- Growth of textile, steel, coal, and shipbuilding industries

- Encouragement of business leaders to find new models of organizing that led to formation of trusts and to the accumulation of capital for innovation, investment, and hiring during and after the war

- The destruction of the Southern economy by federal troops, the ensuing labor shortage because of the end of slavery, and the rise of sharecropping and tenant farming

Complexity Point

- How the growth of giant trusts in the 1880s and 1890s created both positive and negative results for the overall economy

- How opinions differed about ways men who became wealthy during and after the war used their innovations and resources: "robber barons" (selfish and greedy) or "titans of industry" (interested in the well-being of the nation and its people)

- The defeated South's impact on the economy of the entire nation and the rise of the concept of the "New South"

4. Evaluate the impact of the war in Vietnam on United States society in the period 1964 to 1975.

Thesis and Contextualization

At the end of World War II, the United States and the Soviet Union emerged as the dominant world powers. Americans became increasingly concerned about the establishment of Soviet control over and the creation of communist governments in Eastern Europe. As the Cold War evolved, it led to a greater commitment of the United States to contain the spread of communism, especially after the fall of China to communism in 1949. When Nationalist forces with communist leanings defeated the French, Vietnam was divided into North and South, and American presidents took military action to prevent the victory of the North over the South. Thousands of Americans were drafted and sent to Vietnam, especially after 1964. As the war continued and the number of casualties grew, widespread debate on the war's costs, both financial and human, and its lack of progress intensified. Sharp divisions appeared in American society. These divisions were to some extent already present because of political and social controversies over the civil rights movement and the programs of President Johnson's Great Society.

Evidence and Analysis and Reasoning

- The United States policy of containment to prevent the spread of communism (mutual defense pacts such as SEATO, foreign aid to governments trying to resist communism)

- Congress's Gulf of Tonkin Resolution of 1964 giving the president a "blank check" to fight an undeclared war against North Vietnam

- Military draft (Selective Service) and the lottery system limited ways some had used to avoid being drafted

- "A white man's war being fought by black men" argument made by civil rights groups that the war was discriminatory

- Rise of the antiwar movement—youth revolt, draft resistors, Students for a Democratic Society, hippies, antiwar music, Radical Left, counterculture, etc.—that divided American society

- Domestic protest and sometimes violence setting pro-war "hardhats" against antiwar "peaceniks"

Complexity Point

- The connection between the civil rights movement and the antiwar movement

- The divisions over the war contributed to the rise of the Conservative movement in the decades that followed

- How the war and the Watergate scandal of 1972 to 1975 caused distrust of the national government

Use the following table to record where and how you satisfied the rubric and qualified for the point or points.

Long Essay Rubric

Reporting Category	Scoring Criteria
Thesis/Claim (0–1 point) My Thesis	**1 Point:** Responds to the prompt with a historically defensible claim that establishes a line of reasoning.
Contextualization (0–1 point) Identify Contextualization	**1 Point:** Describes a broader historical context relevant to the prompt.
Evidence (0–2 points) List Evidence Identify Argument	**1 Point:** Provides specific examples of evidence relevant to the prompt. **or** **2 Points:** Supports an argument using specific and relevant examples of evidence.
Analysis and Reasoning (0–2 points) Identify Historical Reasoning Identify Complex Understanding	**1 Point:** Uses historical reasoning (comparison, causation, continuity and change. **or** **2 Points:** Demonstrates a **complex understanding** of the historical development that is relevant to the prompt using evidence to corroborate, qualify, or modify an argument that addresses the question.

Practice Exams 1 and 2

Our Practice Exams copy the format of the AP exam as it will be given to you with one important exception: We have included instructions to remind you how to approach the essay questions. Despite this difference, we recommend that you take each Practice Exam under exam time constraints. After you have completed the Practice Exams consider doing the Short-Answer Questions (SAQs) and the Long Essay Questions (LEQs) you did not select for further review of the content and for more practice in writing analytical essays.

Practice Exams 1 and 2

Section	Question Type	Number of Questions	Exam Weight	Timing
I	Multiple-Choice Questions	55	40%	55 minutes
	Short-Answer Questions (Students must answer 1 and 2, then choose either 3 or 4.)	3	20%	40 minutes
II	Document-Based Question	1	25%	60 minutes (includes suggested 15-minute reading period)
	Long Essay Question (Students select 1 of 3 choices.)	1	15%	40 minutes

Practice Exam 1
SECTION I, PART A
Time—55 minutes
55 Questions

Directions: Each of the questions or incomplete statements is followed by four suggested answers or completions. Select the one that is best in each case and then fill in the corresponding answer on the answer sheet provided.

Questions 1 and 2 refer to the following excerpt.

"It is to be understood that the people which now inhabit the regions of the coast of Guinnea, and the midle parts of Africa, as Libya the inner, and Nubia, with divers other great and large regions about the same, were in old time, called Ethiopians and Nigrite, which we now call Moores, Moorens, or Negroes, a people of beastly living, without a God, lawe, religion, or common wealth, and so scorched and vexed with the heat of the sunne, that in many places they curse it when it riseth."

The Second Voyage of M. John Lok to Guinea, Anno 1554

1. In the mid-fifteenth century, Europeans were primarily involved with people of various parts of Africa to

    (A) trade for items such as gold and ivory

    (B) create European colonies in Africa to expand the power of the European kings

    (C) improve the living conditions of African people

    (D) enhance scientific knowledge of the African continent

2. In their contacts with African peoples, the Europeans

    (A) recognized the great diversity among the people of the African continent

    (B) established European-style governments in Africa to introduce European religion and law to African people

    (C) were impressed by the advanced cultures they encountered in Africa

    (D) formed attitudes that led to enslavement of African people

Questions 3–5 refer to the following excerpt.

"So partial are the effects of the system, that its burdens are exclusively on one side and its benefits on the other. It imposes on the agricultural interest of the South, including the Southwest, and that portion of the country particularly engaged in commerce and navigation, the burden not only of sustaining the system itself, but that also of the Government. In stating the case thus strongly, it is not the intention of the committee to exaggerate. If exaggeration were not unworthy of the gravity of the subject, the reality is such as to make it unnecessary.

"[W]e are the serfs of the system, out of whose labor is raised, not only the money paid into the Treasury, but the funds out of which are drawn the rich rewards of the manufacturer and his associates in interest. Their encouragement is our discouragement. The duty on imports, which is mainly paid out of our labor, gives them the means of selling to us at a higher price; while we cannot, to compensate the loss, dispose of our products at the least advance. It is then, indeed, not a subject of wonder, when understood, that our section of the country, though helped by a kind Providence with a genial sun and prolific soil, from which spring the richest products, should languish in poverty and sink into decay, while the rest of the Union, though less fortunate in natural advantages, are flourishing in unexampled prosperity."

John C. Calhoun, South Carolina Exposition and Protest, 1828

3.   The primary purpose of the tax policy that Calhoun was objecting to was to

   (A)   raise revenue for the purpose of the construction of internal improvements

   (B)   protect infant U.S. industries from foreign competition

   (C)   provide subsidies for the construction of the transcontinental railroad

   (D)   construct a modern navy of steel-hulled ships

4.   Ultimately the issues discussed in the South Carolina Exposition led to which of the following?

   (A)   South Carolina nullification of a federal law

   (B)   The impeachment and subsequent acquittal of Andrew Jackson

   (C)   A compromise that provided a dividing line between slave and free states

   (D)   Federal ownership of railroads and steamship lines

5.   John C. Calhoun believed that the federal government was behaving unfairly toward South Carolina by

   (A)   imposing harsh excise taxes on cotton

   (B)   banning the exportation of cotton to foreign countries

   (C)   enacting tax policies that benefited northern industry

   (D)   excessive regulation of agricultural sectors of the economy

Questions 6–8 refer to the following excerpt.

"An Act to provide for the allotment of lands in severalty to Indians on the various reservations, and to extend the protection of the laws of the United States and the Territories over the Indians, and for other purposes.

"Be it enacted by the Senate and House of Representatives of the United States of America in Congress assembled, That in all cases where any tribe or band of Indians has been . . . located upon any reservation created for their use, either by treaty stipulation or by virtue of an act of Congress or executive order setting apart the same for their use, the President of the United States . . . is authorized whenever in his opinion any reservation or any part thereof of such Indians is advantageous for agricultural and grazing purposes, to cause said reservation, or any part thereof, to be surveyed, or resurveyed if necessary, and to allot the lands in said reservation in severalty to any Indian located thereon in quantities as follows:

"To each head of a family, one-quarter of a section. . . ."

The Dawes Act, 1887

6. American Indian advocates who supported the Dawes Act saw it as

   (A) the only way to preserve Indian culture and tribal structure

   (B) the best hope for assimilating Indians into white culture

   (C) a means of acquiring much-needed cash for reservation renovations

   (D) a means of forcing tribes to adjust to an industrial economy

7. The Dawes Act resulted in which of the following?

   (A) The destruction of tribal loyalty and authority

   (B) Industrial training, which led most American Indians to resettle in urban areas

   (C) The opening of additional lands for white settlement

   (D) The destruction of the vast herds of bison on which Plains Indians relied

8. Which of the following was true of the changes in federal policy toward American Indians as the nineteenth century progressed?

   (A) It used military force against Indian tribes for the first time.

   (B) It abandoned the policy of establishing reservations for American Indians.

   (C) It violated many of the treaty guarantees afforded Indians when they ceded their land.

   (D) It committed itself to restoring Indian lands wrongfully taken from tribal ownership.

Questions 9–11 refer to the following excerpt.

"Throughout history, government has proved to be the chief instrument for thwarting man's liberty. Government represents power in the hands of some men to control and regulate the lives of other men.

"State power . . . need not restrict freedom: but absolute state power always does. The *legitimate* functions of government are actually conducive to freedom. Maintaining internal order, keeping foreign foes at bay, administering justice, removing obstacles to the free interchange of goods—the exercise of these powers makes it possible for men to follow their chosen pursuits with maximum freedom. But note that the very instrument by which these desirable ends are achieved *can* be the instrument for achieving undesirable ends—that government can, instead of extending freedom, restrict freedom.

"This is because of the corrupting influence of power, the natural tendency of men who possess *some* power to take unto themselves *more* power. The tendency leads eventually to the acquisition of *all* power—whether in the hands of one or many makes little difference to the freedom of those left on the outside."

Barry Goldwater, *The Conscience of the Conservative*, 1960

9. Senator Barry Goldwater, a leader of the conservative movement of the twentieth century, argued that government power should be

    (A) absolute in order to maintain social and economic order

    (B) limited to the specific powers given to government by the Constitution

    (C) determined by the majority vote of the people

    (D) determined by the legislature of each of the state governments

10. According to the excerpt, a primary function of government was to

    (A) raise tariffs on goods coming into the United States

    (B) create a welfare system so that lower income Americans can have a guaranteed income

    (C) lower taxes on businesses and citizens earning the highest incomes

    (D) provide for the common defense

11. Based on the excerpt, which of the following would Goldwater support?

    (A) The more power the national government has, the more restrictions will be put on the freedom of the people.

    (B) Freedom and liberty of the American people can best be assured by a powerful national government.

    (C) Government in the hands of the wealthiest citizens will assure fair treatment for all Americans.

    (D) The power of the national government should be strong enough to keep the state governments from exercising too much power over the people.

Questions 12–14 refer to the following excerpt

"1. For having, upon specious pretenses of public works, raised great unjust taxes upon the commonalty for the advancement of private favorites and other sinister ends, but no visible effects in any measure adequate; for not having, during this long time of his government, in any measure advanced this hopeful colony either by fortifications, towns, or trade.

. . .

3. For having wronged his Majesty's prerogative and interest by assuming monopoly of the beaver trade and for having in it unjust gain betrayed and sold his Majesty's country and the lives of his loyal subjects to the barbarous heathen.

4. For having protected, favored, and emboldened the Indians against his Majesty's loyal subjects, never contriving, requiring, or appointing any due or proper means of satisfaction for their many invasions, robberies, and murders committed upon us.

. . .

6. And lately, when, upon the loud outcries of blood, the assembly had, with all care, raised and framed an army for the preventing of further mischief and safeguard of this his Majesty's colony.

Of this and the aforesaid articles we accuse Sir William Berkeley as guilty of each and every one of the same, and as one who has traitorously attempted, violated, and injured his Majesty's interest here by a loss of a great part of this his colony and many of his faithful loyal subjects by him betrayed and in a barbarous and shameful manner exposed to the incursions and murder of the heathen. . .Nathaniel Bacon"

"Declaration of Nathaniel Bacon in the Name of the People of Virginia, July 30, 1676."

12.   Bacon's rebellion best exemplifies which of the following conflicts in the British North American colonies?

(A)   Conflict between colonial assemblies and Parliament

(B)   Conflict between colonial militia and the regular British army

(C)   Conflict between the tidewater and the backcountry

(D)   Conflict between northern and southern colonies

13.   Concerns over the makeup of Bacon's army led to

(A)   introduction of a system of land distribution in colonial Virginia

(B)   institutionalization of the system of forced labor in Virginia

(C)   the Anglican Church becoming tax supported throughout the British North American colonies

(D)   British attempts to end salutary neglect through the creation of the Dominion of New England

14.   The passage above suggests that Bacon was most concerned with

(A)   unfair taxes imposed on Virginia by Great Britain

(B)   failure of the colonial government to provide adequate protection from Indian raids

(C)   trade restrictions placed on the colonies by the Trade and Navigation Acts

(D)   failure of the British government to provide assurances of religious freedom

Questions 15–18 refer to the following excerpt.

"Such . . . is the language held towards us and ours. The peculiar institutions of the South . . . [are] pronounced to be sinful and odious, in the sight of God and man; and this with a systematic design of rendering us hateful in the eyes of the world, with a view to a general crusade against us and our institutions. This too, in the legislative halls of the Union . . . we . . . are expected to sit here in silence, hearing ourselves and our constituents day after day denounced . . . if we but open our lips, the charge of agitation is resounded on all sides. . . . Every reflecting mind must see in this, a state of things deeply and dangerously diseased. . .

"[Those enslaved have] attained a condition so civilised and so improved, not only physically but morally and intellectually. . .in the course of a few generations it has grown up under the fostering care of our institutions, as reviled as they have been, to its present comparative civilised condition. . . .

"I hold that in the present state of civilization, where two races of different origin [are brought together] the relation now existing in the slaveholding States between the two, is, instead of an evil, a good—a positive good. I feel myself called upon to speak freely upon the subject where the honour and interests of those I represent are involved."

John C. Calhoun, Speech in Congress, February 6, 1837

15. How did John C. Calhoun's speech represent a significant turning point in Southerners' explanation and defense of slavery?

    (A) He recognized the validity of much of the criticism the South received from those who opposed slavery.

    (B) He represented the views of those who were enslaved and had no political representation themselves.

    (C) He called on those living in the rest of the country to recognize that slavery was essential for the Southern economy.

    (D) He described slavery as a benevolent institution that operated for the good of those enslaved.

16. Why did Southerners like Calhoun feel the need to speak out in defense of slavery?

    (A) Abolitionist activities were increasing in the North, and many Southerners feared the possibility of slave uprisings.

    (B) The South was industrializing rapidly and felt it needed slavery in order to supply cotton for their new textile mills.

    (C) The numbers of free blacks in the South had increased dramatically, and many Southerners feared an increased call for abolition.

    (D) Southern churches were united against the institution of slavery because it raised tensions within the regions.

17.   What did Calhoun mean when he described slavery as "the peculiar institution"?

(A)   He acknowledged that slavery was an institution that no one would be able to understand.

(B)   He argued that slavery was an institution that was unique to the South.

(C)   He admitted that slavery was a practice that could not be condoned by those of any religion.

(D)   He made the claim that slavery was both evil and a positive good.

18.   How did this new approach to justifying slavery affect national politics in the decades leading up to the Civil War?

(A)   Many Northern abolitionists were willing to admit that there were some positive aspects to the slave system.

(B)   Southern members of Congress organized speaking tours throughout the northern states to help people understand the southern point of view.

(C)   Southerners became increasingly defensive and resistant to any efforts to limit the expansion of slave holders' rights.

(D)   Northern manufacturers began to lobby Congress to provide more money for Southern industrial development as slave labor became more widely acceptable.

Questions 19–22 refer to the following excerpt.

"Mankind being originally equals in the order of creation, the equality could only be destroyed by some circumstance; the distinctions of rich, and poor, may in great measure be accounted for. . . . But there is another and greater distinction for which no truly natural or religious reason can be assigned, and that is, the distinction of men into KINGS and SUBECTS. . . . To the evil of monarchy, we have added that of hereditary succession . . . an insult and an imposition on posterity. For all men being originally equals, no one by birth could have a right to set up his own family in perpetual preference to all others for ever. . . . The nearer a government approaches to a republic the less business there is for a king. It is somewhat difficult to find a proper name for the government of England. Sir William Meredith calls it a republic; but in its present state it is unworthy of the name, because of the corrupt influence of the crown. . . . It is the republican and not the monarchical part of the constitution of England which Englishmen glory in . . . the liberty of choosing a house of commons from out of their own body—and it is easy to see that when republican virtue fails, slavery ensues."

Thomas Paine, *Common Sense*, 1776

19. According to this excerpt, what did Thomas Paine feel was one of the illogical sorts of inequality faced by mankind?

    (A) The differences in the lives of the rich and the poor

    (B) The distinction made between a monarch and those whom a monarch ruled

    (C) The failure to recognize the value of hereditary succession of monarchs

    (D) The structure of a government that divides power between two houses

20. What did Paine feel was one of the chief benefits of a republican form of government?

    (A) Paine believed only a republic allowed men to be able to decide for themselves the best form of government.

    (B) Paine felt a republican form of government eliminated the need for a monarch.

    (C) Paine believed the British Parliament was the best illustration of the effectiveness of a republican government.

    (D) Paine maintained that a republican form of government kept the influence of religion out of politics.

21. Why did Paine feel the government of Great Britain was not worthy of being labeled a "republic"?

    (A) British citizens did not get to choose their representatives in any sort of direct elections.

    (B) He believed a true republic could not exist if a nation still had wide gaps between the rich and the poor.

    (C) Paine felt the monarchy had too much influence over the government to allow Britain to be truly an example of a republic.

    (D) He felt the House of Commons should be more supportive of the hereditary monarchy.

22. How did Paine's argument illustrate the influence of Enlightenment philosophy on his position?

    (A) Enlightenment philosophers believed that men should be able to choose their own governments and change them when they no longer served the general interest.

    (B) The leaders of the Enlightenment felt society should be organized in such a way that poverty was eliminated and all men had equal property.

    (C) Enlightenment thinkers felt monarchy was generally a positive form of government, so long as there were limits to hereditary power.

    (D) Most Enlightenment thinkers felt organized governments would never be successful because men were selfish and argumentative by nature.

Questions 23–25 refer to the following excerpt.

"The eighth wonder of the world is this: two pounds of iron-stone purchased on the shores of Lake Superior and transported to Pittsburgh; two pounds of coal mined in Connellsville and manufactured into coke and brought to Pittsburgh; one half pound of limestone mined east of the Alleghenies and brought to Pittsburgh; a little manganese ore, mined in Virginia and brought to Pittsburgh. And these four- and one-half pounds of material manufactured into one pound of solid steel and sold for one cent. That's all that need be said about the steel business."

Andrew Carnegie, "Ode to Steelmaking," from Harold Livesay,
Andrew Carnegie and the Rise of Big Business.

23. The successful employment of the strategy described by Andrew Carnegie allowed business leaders to

   (A) successfully extract subsidies from the national government

   (B) gain significant shares of the market in various industries

   (C) dictate the foreign policy of the U.S. government

   (D) ignore wage and price controls

24. Entrepreneurs who amassed great fortunes generally

   (A) paid high wages to prevent the organization of labor unions and avoid strikes

   (B) tended to avoid the ostentatious displays of their wealth

   (C) actively petitioned the government for fair trade practices legislation

   (D) sought to eliminate competition through a number of sometimes ruthless methods

25. Carnegie's vision of the responsibility of the wealthy held that

   (A) it was the duty of the United States to conquer economically backward civilizations

   (B) God entrusted them with wealth because they knew how to best use the money for the common good

   (C) they should flaunt their wealth as an encouragement to the poor to work hard

   (D) they should donate their excess revenue to federal government welfare programs

Questions 26–28 refer to the following image.

"Be Sure To Give Mine Special Attention"

Washington Post, 1955, Herblock. Rosenwald Collection

26. The above political cartoon best depicted which of the following phenomenon of the late 1940s and 1950s?

    (A) Fear of communist infiltration into the public school systems of the United States

    (B) The definitive movement toward the employment of women to gain two-parent incomes

    (C) The proliferation of children as a result of the postwar baby boom

    (D) Desegregation of public schools following *Brown v. Board of Education*

27. The above political cartoon implied which of the following about the role of children in the 1950s?

    (A) Children formed the bulwark against communist cold war infiltration into the United States

    (B) Children took a backseat in importance to their parent's desire for a two-parent income

    (C) Education of children diminished in importance as threats of atomic warfare increased

    (D) Parents elevated the importance of children by indicating they were the best and the brightest

28. When the population cohort born between 1946 and 1963 reached childbearing years, they

    (A) had children later in life and fewer in number than the previous generation

    (B) exploded a population bomb that doubled the U.S. population in a single generation

    (C) insured Democratic dominance of the presidency for the next 25 years

    (D) ceased to be a cause of societal readjustment to accommodate their numbers

Questions 29–31 refer to the following image.

Leftycartoons by Barry Deutsch

29. What was a common fear about immigrants expressed in the cartoon above?

    (A) People feared immigrants brought contagious diseases to the United States from their countries of origin.

    (B) Many people feared newly arriving immigrants would undercut wages for American workers.

    (C) Most people believed immigrants were not willing to work and would create huge welfare expenses.

    (D) Few immigrants practiced any organized religion, so many people felt they had no moral conscience.

30. What is ironic about the persistence of nativism in American society since the nation's founding?

    (A) The United States has always been a nation whose existence was based on immigration.

    (B) The United States had open immigration laws in the nineteenth and twentieth centuries.

    (C) Immigrant labor has never been a significant factor in U.S. employment figures.

    (D) Anti-immigration sentiments were always based on economic issues rather than cultural or religious ones.

31.   Which of the following groups might offer the strongest argument against the validity of this nativism in American society?

   (A)   Spanish conquistadors, who were living in the Americas before the British settlers

   (B)   Native Americans, who were the original inhabitants of North America

   (C)   French trappers and traders, who lived in relative harmony with Native Americans

   (D)   Portuguese sailors, who launched the first efforts at European colonization

Questions 32–34 refer to the following excerpt.

"Question I.—*Who are the Subjects of Baptism?*
The Answer may be given in the following *propositions*, briefly confirmed from the Scriptures.
"1. They that, according to Scripture, are members of the visible church, are the subjects of baptism.
"2. The members of the visible church, according to Scripture, are confederate visible Believers, in particular churches, and their infant seed, *i. e.* children in minority, whose next parents, one or both, are in covenant.
"3. The infant seed of confederate visible believers, are members of the same church with their parents, and when grown up are personally under the watch, discipline and government of that church.
"4. These adult persons are not therefore to be admitted to full Communion, merely because they are, and continue members, without such further qualifications as the word of God requireth thereunto.
"5. Church members who were admitted in minority, understanding the doctrine of faith, and publickly professing their assent thereto, not scandalous in life, and solemnly owning the covenant before the church, wherein they give up themselves and their children to the Lord, and subject themselves to the government of Christ in the church, their children are to be baptised."

The Results of the Three Synods, Assembled at Boston in the Year 1662

32. The above excerpt would suggest which of the following concerning Puritan influence in New England?

    (A) Puritans were increasingly concerned with the influx of Quakers into the colony.

    (B) Puritans were committed to the separation of church and state and the concept of freedom of religion.

    (C) Puritans sought to mitigate the Salem Witch Trial's exposure of witches as Puritan church members.

    (D) Puritans were concerned with declining influence and thus eased requirements for church membership.

33. The above excerpt is most commonly referred to as which of the following?

    (A) The New England Confederation

    (B) *A Model of Christian Charity*

    (C) *Sinners in the Hands of an Angry God*

    (D) The Halfway Covenant

34. Puritan intolerance of other religions led most directly to

    (A) the rapid depopulation of Massachusetts Bay

    (B) an emotional religious revival that swept the colonies in the mid-18th century

    (C) the expulsion of religious dissenters from the colony

    (D) the revocation of their charter by the English government

Questions 35–37 refer to the following excerpt.

"So for generations in the mind of America, the Negro has been more of a formula than a human being—a something to be argued about, condemned or defended, to be 'kept down,' or 'in his place,' or 'helped up,' to be worried with or worried over, harassed or patronized, a social bogey or a social burden. . . . The migrant masses, shifting from countryside to city, hurdle several generations of experience at a leap, but more important, the same thing happens spiritually in the life-attitudes and self-expression of the Young Negro, in his poetry, his art, his education and his new outlook. . . .

The Negro today is inevitably moving forward under the control largely of his own objectives. . . . Democracy itself is obstructed and stagnated to the extent that any of its channels are closed. Indeed they cannot be selectively closed. So the choice is not between one way for the Negro and another way for the rest, but between American institutions frustrated on the one hand and American ideals progressively fulfilled and realized on the other.

"The pulse of the Negro world has begun to beat in Harlem. A Negro newspaper carrying news material in English, French and Spanish, gathered from all quarters of America, the West Indies and Africa has maintained itself in Harlem for over five years. . . . And certainly, if in our lifetime the Negro should not be able to celebrate his full initiation into American democracy, he can at least, on the warrant of these things, celebrate the attainment of a significant and satisfying new phase of group development, and with it a spiritual Coming of Age."

Alain Locke, "Enter the New Negro," *Survey Graphic* (March 1925)

35. Which of the following constituted Alain Locke's vision of what he called "the New Negro" in the 1920s?

    (A) Locke was celebrating a general lifting of the segregationist Jim Crow policies that had been such a large part of Southern politics and culture in the nineteenth century.

    (B) He felt that most discrimination facing African Americans in the United States would vanish within his own lifetime.

    (C) He saw African Americans as refusing to recognize old stereotypes and demanding to be allowed to think and act on their own.

    (D) Locke saw a change coming to African American youth as they learned to speak other languages.

36. What shift in American society did Locke see as having contributed in part to this new attitude on the part of many African Americans?

    (A) He credited the Great Migration out of the South to the North and Midwest as opening up African American perspectives to a world beyond Jim Crow.

    (B) He believed that most Americans finally realized that all American institutions have to offer equal access to people regardless of race.

    (C) Newspapers designed and published for African American communities did not exist until the 1920s.

    (D) More American reformers and philanthropists were looking for ways to help African American communities throughout the nation.

37. Why did Locke single out Harlem as "the pulse of the Negro world" at this period of American history?

(A) Harlem was an example of a fully integrated and multicultural urban area, and Locke thought it would be an example for the rest of the country.

(B) Harlem in New York City became a central focus of the Great Migration, resulting in a cultural phenomenon that came to be known as the "Harlem Renaissance."

(C) Harlem was a major industrial and manufacturing center, and African Americans were able to find good paying jobs there.

(D) Philanthropists in Harlem organized programs and provided funds throughout the South to encourage families to move North.

Questions 38–40 refer to the following excerpt.

"Here are no aristocratic families, no courts, no kings, no bishops, no ecclesiastical dominion, no invisible power giving to a few a very visible one, no great manufacturers employing thousands, no great refinements of luxury. The rich and poor are not so far removed from each other as they are in Europe. . . . They are a mixture of English, Scotch, Irish, French, Dutch, Germans, and Swedes. From this promiscuous breed, that race now called Americans have arisen. . . . Every thing has tended to regenerate them; new laws, a new mode of living, a new social system; here they are become men. . . . Formerly they were not numbered in any civil lists of their country, except in those of the poor; here they rank as citizens. . . . What then is the American? This new man? He is either an European, or the descendant of an European, hence that strange mixture of blood, which you will find in no other country. . . . Here individuals of all nations are melted into a new race of men, whose labours and posterity will one day cause great changes in the world.

J. Hector St. John Crevecoeur, "What Is an American?"
Letters from an American Farmer, Letter III (1782)

38. What was Crevecoeur's point about the people who made up the new America in the wake of the American Revolution?

    (A) All of those living in the United States owed their prosperity to the fact that they came from Europe originally.

    (B) Citizens of the new United States generally lacked the social graces of those who lived In Europe.

    (C) Those living in the new United States experienced a degree of social equality and freedom that was not available in Europe.

    (D) There were no poor people living in the United States, as there were in most European Countries.

39. What did Crevecoeur consider the primary factors in the emergence of this new group of people?

    (A) They had been able to learn other languages as they originally came from so many different countries.

    (B) They had been able to remake their lives without the restrictions of European social, civil, and economic restrictions.

    (C) The American economy benefited from having a strong manufacturing and industrial base of its own.

    (D) Most of the immigrants to North America came from continental Europe rather than Great Britain.

40. What factor was overlooked in Crevecoeur's positive view of the society emerging in the aftermath of the Revolution?

    (A) He did not mention the financial strength of the new nation's government.

    (B) He failed to note that all the adult men in the new nation were allowed to vote in national elections.

    (C) He overlooked praise for the insistence on religious toleration enjoyed by all those living in the new country.

    (D) He did not acknowledge the existence of a large number of enslaved people in the new nation.

Questions 41-43 refer to the following excerpt.

"ANALYSIS

I. Background of the Present Crisis

Within the past thirty-five years the world has experienced two global wars of tremendous violence. . . .

For several centuries it had proved impossible for any one nation to gain such preponderant strength that a coalition of other nations could not in time face it with greater strength. . . .

Two complex sets of factors have now basically altered this historic distribution of power. First, the defeat of Germany and Japan and the decline of the British and French Empires have interacted with the development of the United States and the Soviet Union in such a way that power increasingly gravitated to these two centers. Second, the Soviet Union, unlike previous aspirants to hegemony, is animated by a new fanatic faith, antithetical to our own, and seeks to impose its absolute authority over the rest of the world. Conflict has, therefore, become endemic and is waged, on the part of the Soviet Union, by violent or non-violent methods in accordance with the dictates of expediency. With the development of increasingly terrifying weapons of mass destruction, every individual faces the ever-present possibility of annihilation should the conflict enter the phase of total war.

IX. Possible Courses of Action

Introduction. Four possible courses of action by the United States in the present situation can be distinguished. They are:

    a. Continuation of current policies, with current and currently projected programs for carrying out these policies;

    b. Isolation;

    c. War; and

    d. A more rapid building up of the political, economic, and military strength of the free world than provided under a, with the purpose of reaching, if possible, a tolerable state of order among nations without war and of preparing to defend ourselves in the event that the free world is attacked."

         NSC 68: United States Objectives and Programs for National Security, April 14, 1950

41. The above document was, in part, a reaction to which of the following?

    (A) The successful development of atomic weapons by the Soviet Union

    (B) The defeat of the French colonial empire in Southeast Asia

    (C) The failure of Western European countries to accept U.S. economic aid following World War II

    (D) The need for economic recovery following the Great Depression

42. Which of the following resulted from the recommendations made by NSC 68?

    (A) Direct military confrontation between the United States and the Soviet Union in Vietnam

    (B) The rollback of communist gains made by the Soviet Union in Eastern Europe following World War II

    (C) An arms race between the United States and the Soviet Union that led to fears of mutually assured destruction

    (D) Determination of the United States to resume its traditional foreign policy of isolationism

43. In his farewell address, President Eisenhower warned the country of which of the following dangers?

    (A) U.S. adherence to the policy of peaceful coexistence with the Soviet Union

    (B) U.S. policy of détente with the Soviet Union

    (C) The power of the military/industrial complex in the United States

    (D) Negotiating with the Soviet Union concerning limiting atmospheric nuclear testing

Questions 44–46 refer to the following map.

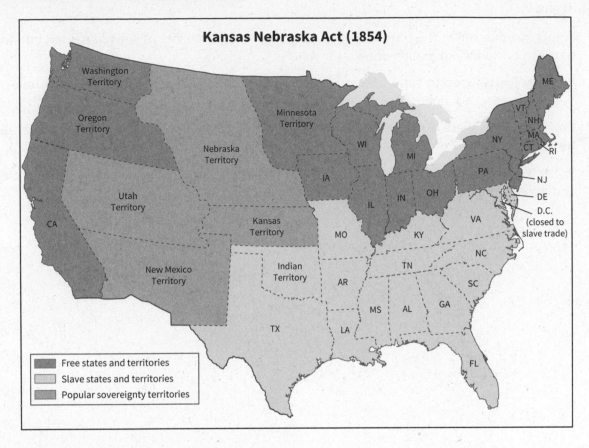

44. What federal legislation was invalidated by the Kansas-Nebraska Act of 1854?

    (A) The Louisiana Purchase of 1803

    (B) The Treaty of Guadalupe-Hidalgo of 1846

    (C) The Missouri Compromise of 1820

    (D) The Indian Removal Act of 1830

45. How did eastern abolitionists react to the concept of popular sovereignty?

    (A) They felt it was a fair way to decide the issue of the expansion of slavery because popular sovereignty was based on democratic principles.

    (B) They were opposed to any legislation that resulted in the addition of new slave territories or states to the Union.

    (C) They did not like the concept but accepted it as the only way to keep the Union together.

    (D) They took no position on popular sovereignty as they were convinced the climate and geography of the territories involved were unsuitable for slavery.

46. What were the consequences of the provision of allowing popular sovereignty in Kansas and Nebraska after 1854?

    (A) Fighting broke out in the territories as supporters and opponents of slavery rushed into the area to try to sway the upcoming votes.

    (B) Southerners refused to support popular sovereignty as they felt the Great Plains were unsuitable for slave-based agriculture.

    (C) Both territories were quickly settled, with Kansas becoming a slave territory and Nebraska becoming a free territory.

    (D) While there was some unrest in the territories themselves, members of Congress were pleased and agreed that the issue of slavery was being decided fairly.

Questions 47–49 refer to the following excerpt.

"But the most important effect of the frontier has been in the promotion of democracy here and in Europe. As has been indicated the frontier is productive of individualism. Complex society is precipitated by the wilderness into a kind of primitive organization, based on the family. . . . The frontier individualism has from the beginning promoted democracy. . . . So long as free land exists, the opportunity for a competency exists, and economic power secures political power. . . . From the conditions of frontier life came intellectual traits of profound importance. . . . The result is that to the frontier the American intellect owes its striking characteristics. That coarseness and strength combined with acuteness and inquisitiveness; that practical, inventive turn of mind, quick to find expedients . . . that restless, nervous energy; that dominant individualism, working for good and for evil, and withal that buoyancy and exuberance which comes with freedom—these are traits of the frontier, or traits called out elsewhere because of the existence of the frontier. . . . And now, four centuries from the discovery of America, at the end of a hundred years of life under the Constitution, the frontier has gone, and with its going has closed the first period of American history."

Frederick Jackson Turner, *The Significance of the Frontier in American History*, 1893

47. What led to Turner's presentation on the importance of the frontier in the history of the United States?

   (A) Turner was disturbed by the disappearance of American Indian tribes, and he wanted to encourage settlers to remember that the frontier had to have room for all.

   (B) The 1890 U.S. Census had found that an open frontier no longer existed in the United States, and Turner felt that would have an impact on national development.

   (C) Turner felt that a majority of the people in the United States had forgotten the democratic principles on which the nation was founded.

   (D) Turner was concerned that too much emphasis on individualism would lead people to forget that democracy meant all should be represented equally in government.

48. What were the implications of Turner's thesis on the nation's devotion to the concept of Manifest Destiny, which was such a big part of nineteenth-century expansion?

   (A) If the country still needed to expand in order to continue to develop power and wealth, new frontiers would have to be found outside of the continent.

   (B) Once the frontier was closed, the concept of expansion justified by the ideals of Manifest Destiny would no longer be a part of the American experience.

   (C) Turner, like many in the nineteenth century, felt the ideas behind Manifest Destiny had led pioneers to take unfair advantage of the Indian tribes who already lived on the frontier.

   (D) The view of Manifest Destiny shifted from advocating expansion to one that focused exclusively on economic and industrial development.

49. What aspects of western expansion were missing from Turner's evaluation of the importance of a frontier as a part of the development of the United States?

    (A) He did not see any connection between expansion in the west and the growth of industrialism and economic power in the rest of the country.

    (B) He saw no connection between the growth of political awareness on the frontier and the development of political institutions in general.

    (C) He felt that individualism was uniformly a positive characteristic that could have no downside in the country's development.

    (D) Turner overlooked the many aspects of frontier expansion that were not positive or democratic, such as the elimination of Indian nations and destruction of the buffalo.

Questions 50–52 refer to the following excerpt.

"If the opinion of the Supreme Court covered the whole ground of this act, it ought not to control the coordinate authorities of this Government. The Congress, the Executive, and the Court must each for itself be guided by its own opinion of the Constitution. Each public officer who takes an oath to support the Constitution swears that he will support it as he understands it, and not as it is understood by others. It is as much the duty of the House of Representatives, of the Senate, and of the President to decide upon the constitutionality of any bill or resolution which may be presented to them for passage or approval as it is of the supreme judges when it may be brought before them for judicial decision. The opinion of the judges has no more authority over Congress than the opinion of Congress has over the judges, and on that point the President is independent of both. The authority of the Supreme Court must not, therefore, be permitted to control the Congress or the Executive when acting in their legislative capacities, but to have only such influence as the force of their reasoning may deserve."

> Andrew Jackson's Veto Message to the Re-Chartering of the
> Bank of the United States, 1832

50. Jackson was challenging which of the following principles in the above passage?

    (A)   The principle that the U.S. Senate had exclusive treaty-making power

    (B)   The exclusive right of Congress to enact protective tariffs to benefit infant industries

    (C)   The right of Congress to ban the extension of slavery into the territories

    (D)   The principle that the power of judicial review applied only to the courts

51. Which of the following best represented the increased use of presidential power during the Jacksonian era?

    (A)   Movement toward a civil service system based on merit

    (B)   Military incursions into Florida to force the Spanish to sell the territory

    (C)   Setting in motion the forced removal of eastern woodland tribes

    (D)   Executive reallocation of funds for the construction of the Erie Canal

52. The Era of Jacksonian Democracy witnessed which of the following?

    (A)   Democratization of the political process

    (B)   Ratification of the Thirteenth Amendment banning slavery

    (C)   Establishment of a state church following the Second Great Awakening

    (D)   Federally funded reform movements for temperance and public education

Questions 53–55 refer to the following song.

Little boxes on the hillside,
Little boxes made of ticky tacky,
Little boxes on the hillside,
Little boxes all the same.
There's a green one and a pink one
And a blue one and a yellow one,
And they're all made out of ticky tacky
And they all look just the same.

And the people in the houses
All went to the university,
Where they were put in boxes
And they came out all the same,
And there's doctors and lawyers,
And business executives,
And they're all made out of ticky tacky
And they all look just the same.

And they all play on the golf course
And drink their martinis dry,
And they all have pretty children
And the children go to school,
And the children go to summer camp
And then to the university,
Where they are put in boxes
And they come out all the same.

And the boys go into business
And marry and raise a family
In boxes made of ticky tacky
And they all look just the same.
There's a green one and a pink one
And a blue one and a yellow one,
And they're all made out of ticky tacky
And they all look just the same.

"Little Boxes," Malvina Reynolds, 1962
Words and music by Malvina Reynolds; copyright 1962 Schroder Music Company

53. Which of the following was the focus of Malvina Reynolds' attack in the song "Little Boxes"?

(A) The anti-war demonstrators of the 1960s which she viewed as unpatriotic

(B) The "beat generation's" support of McCarthyism during the Red Scare

(C) The second feminist wave's opposition to the reemergence of the cult of domesticity

(D) The conformist and materialistic mass society of the 1950s

54. "Little Boxes" is most closely related to which of the following developments of the time period?

(A) The growing suburbanization of the United States exemplified by Levittowns

(B) The growing demand for an Equal Rights Amendment by the women's liberation movement

(C) The cold war's insistence on anti-communist sentiment

(D) The transformation from an industrial-based to a service-based economy

55. Reynolds, criticism of American society most nearly mirrors the themes of which of the previous groups of American writers?

(A) The muckraker's exposés concerning the societal ills and business practices in the early 1900s

(B) Female serialized romantic novelists of the 1840s and 1850s empowering women by rejecting the notion of "separate spheres"

(C) Transcendental writers who rejected reason in favor of intuition and experience

(D) The lost generation's attacks on the superficiality nature of American society during the 1920

CHAPTER FOUR : PRACTICE EXAMS 1 AND 2

AT THIS POINT ON THE ACTUAL EXAM,
YOU WOULD BE ALLOWED TO CHECK WORK ON PART A,
BUT NOT CONTINUE ON TO PART B.

Multiple-Choice Answer Sheet

1. _____	20. _____	39. _____
2. _____	21. _____	40. _____
3. _____	22. _____	41. _____
4. _____	23. _____	42. _____
5. _____	24. _____	43. _____
6. _____	25. _____	44. _____
7. _____	26. _____	45. _____
8. _____	27. _____	46. _____
9. _____	28. _____	47. _____
10. _____	29. _____	48. _____
11. _____	30. _____	49. _____
12. _____	31. _____	50. _____
13. _____	32. _____	51. _____
14. _____	33. _____	52. _____
15. _____	34. _____	53. _____
16. _____	35. _____	54. _____
17. _____	36. _____	55. _____
18. _____	37. _____	
19. _____	38. _____	

CHAPTER FOUR : PRACTICE EXAMS 1 AND 2

Practice Exam 1
SECTION I, PART B
Time—40 minutes

Directions: Answer Question 1 **and** Question 2. Answer **either** Question 3 **or** Question 4.

Write your response to each question on the lined page designated for that response. Each response is expected to fit within the space provided.

In your responses, be sure to address all parts of the questions you answer. Use complete sentences; an outline or bulleted list alone is not acceptable. You should write your answers on the appropriate blank answer sheets provided below. **Note: No credit will be given on the exam for responses in the wrong location.**

Short-Answer Question 1

"The utopia of the Populists was in the past, not in the future. According to the agrarian myth, the health of the state was proportionate to the degree to which it was dominated by the agricultural class, and this assumption pointed to the superiority of an earlier age. . . .

"[A time] when there were few millionaires . . . when the laborer had excellent prospects and the farmer had abundance. . . .

"What they meant . . . was that they would like to restore the conditions prevailing before the development of industrialism and the commercialization of agriculture."

Richard Hofstadter, *The Age of Reform,* 1955

"Populism was a progressive social force. It accepted industrial society, posed solutions not seeking to turn back the clock, and was strongly pro-labor.

"Not only did Populism look forward rather than backward, but it also was deeply committed to freedom. It attacked the very character of industrial capitalist society. . . .

"Industrial America must be altered in a truly democratic direction.

"Populism was more than a protest movement; it was a glorious chapter in the eternal struggle for human rights."

Norman Pollack, *The Populist Response to Industrial America*,
New York: W.W. Norton & Company, Inc., 1966, p. 143.

1. Using the excerpts above, answer (a), (b), and (c).

    a) Briefly describe ONE important difference between Hofstadter's and Pollock's historical interpretation of the goals of the Populists at the end of the nineteenth century.

    b) Briefly explain how ONE specific historical event, development, or circumstance in the late nineteenth century created a threat to the American farmer leading to the Populists' goals described by Hofstadter.

    c) Briefly explain how ONE specific political or economic reform supported by the Populists in the late nineteenth and early twentieth century attempted to accomplish their goals as described by Pollock.

Short-Answer Question 2

The World's Plunderers

Thomas Nast, 1885   Betman/Getty Images

2.   Using the image above, answer (a), (b), and (c).

   a)   Briefly describe what the image illustrates about European nations in the last part of the nineteenth century.

   b)   Briefly explain how the actions of the European nations illustrated in the image had an impact on U.S. foreign policy.

   c)   Briefly describe ONE specific example of how the United States responded to the situation depicted in the image.

Directions: Answer **either** Question 3 **or** Question 4.

Short-Answer Question 3

3. Answer (a), (b), and (c). Confine your response to the period from 1491 to 1607.

    a) Briefly describe how ONE specific aspect of the lives of the natives in the Mississippi River Valley were influenced by the geography and environment of the region.

    b) Briefly describe how ONE specific aspect of the lives of the natives in the Great Plains were influenced by the geography and environment of the region.

    c) Briefly describe how ONE specific aspect of the lives of the natives of the woodlands of northeastern North America were influenced the geography and environment of the region.

Short-Answer Question 4

4. Answer (a), (b), and (c).

    a) Briefly explain ONE specific cause for changes in the natural environment and the supply of natural resources of the United States during the 1968–1980 period.

    b) Briefly explain ONE specific action taken to alleviate the negative aspects of changes to the environment and supply of resources of the United States during the 1968–1980 period.

    c) Briefly describe ONE specific example of how environmental factors and needs for resources influenced U.S. actions in other parts of the world during the 1968–1980 period.

Short-Answer Response Sheets

Question 1

_____
_____
_____
_____
_____
_____
_____
_____
_____
_____
_____
_____
_____
_____
_____
_____
_____
_____
_____
_____
_____
_____
_____
_____
_____
_____
_____
_____
_____

Question 2

Question 3

Question 4

SECTION II: FREE-RESPONSE QUESTIONS
Practice Exam 1
Total Time—1 hour and 40 minutes
Question 1 (Document-Based Question)
Suggested reading and writing time: 1 hour

It is suggested that you spend 15 minutes reading the documents and 45 minutes writing your response on additional paper. You will be provided an answer booklet when you take the AP examination.

Note: You may begin writing your response before the reading period is over.

Directions: Question 1 is based on the accompanying documents. The documents have been edited for the purpose of this exercise.

In your response you should do the following:

- Respond to the prompt with a historically defensible thesis or claim that establishes a line of reasoning.

- Describe a broader historical context relevant to the prompt.

- Support an argument in response to the prompt using at least six documents.

- Use at least one additional piece of specific historical evidence (beyond that found in the documents) relevant to an argument about the prompt.

- For at least three documents, explain how or why the document's point of view, purpose, historical situation, and/or audience is relevant to an argument.

- Use evidence to corroborate, qualify, or modify an argument that addresses the prompt.

1. **Evaluate the extent to which ideas about the distribution of political power shaped the structure and function of the federal government in the period 1783 to 1800.**

Document 1

Source: Bernard Bailyn, "On Rereading the Ideological Origins," *New England Quarterly* 91(2018): 29–31.

The fear of power did not end with Independence. It carried through the complicated process by which the states formed or reformed their provincial constitutions and dominated the ratification of the national constitution.

* * *

In that great national struggle, every clause of the Constitution and every conceivable ramification was scoured for possible consequences. . . . The country's best minds bent to the effort to approve or disapprove, of the Constitution as it had been submitted by the Convention of 1787. And in this they faced a bewildering dilemma that derived from the still dominant fear of power. Many of the state and national leaders—not all, but some of the most influential—knew the absolute necessity to create a forceful power center in the new national government that would replace the loose and ineffective "league of friendship" defined by the Articles of Confederation. In the six years under the Articles, the basic stability of the nation, largely in the hands of state governments, had come under pressure from populist forces and local interests that threatened not only the welfare of local property owners and defenders of the rule of law but also from those of broader vision who hoped that the nation would play an effective national power over the states and their people would have to be created. But to construct a new national power center when a war had just been fought to defy such a force flew directly into the face of the ideology that had stirred American resistance a decade earlier.

Document 2

Source: Henry Knox, the War Office, to Congress, September 28, 1786, *Journals of the Continental Congress, 1774–1789*, ed. John Fitzpatrick (Washington, DC: Government Printing Office, 1934), 32: 698–699.

At the time I wrote to the Governor from Springfield the height to which the disorders might arise were uncertain. Enough of a lawless and desperate spirit had been manifested to alarm the well affected to Government.

* * *

Beside the danger before alluded to in calling out a body of militia for the security of Springfield, the expense of subsisting them would be considerable, and must be defrayed by the United States, which if practicable would greatly embarrass the Treasury

Were there a respectable body of troops in the service of the United States as to be ordered immediately to Springfield, the propriety of the measure could not be doubted. Or were the finances of the United States in such order as to enable Congress to raise an additional body of four or five hundred men and station them at the respective arsenals the spirit of the times would highly justify the measure.

Document 3

Source: Richard Henry Lee, October 8, 1787, *Letters from the Federal Farmer to the Republican*, Thomas Greenleaf, 1787

The plan of government now proposed is evidently calculated totally to change, in time, our condition as a people. Instead of being thirteen republics, under a federal head, it is clearly designed to make us one consolidated government. . . . This consolidation of states has been the object of several men in this country for some time past. . . . whether such a change will not totally destroy the liberties of this country—time only can determine.

The confederation was formed when great confidence was placed in the voluntary exertions of individuals, and of the respective states; and the framers of it, to guard against usurpations, so limited and checked the powers, that, in many respects, they are inadequate to the exigencies of the union. We find therefore, members of congress urging alterations in the federal system almost as soon as it was adopted. It was early proposed to vest congress with power to levy an impost, to regulate trade, &c but such was known to be the cause of the states in parting with power, that the vestment, even of these, was proposed to be under several checks and limitations. . . . And should an oppressive government be the consequence of the proposed change, posterity may reproach not only a few overbearing unprincipled men.

Document 4

Source: Publius, *Federalist 21*, December 12, 1787

The United States as now composed, have no power to exact obedience, or punish disobedience to their resolutions, either by pecuniary mulcts [fines] by a suspension or divestiture of privileges, or by any other constitutional means. There is no express delegation of authority to them to use force against delinquent members; and if such a right should be ascribed to the federal head, . . . it must be by inference and construction, in the face of that part of the second article in which it is declared, "that each state shall retain every power, jurisdiction and right, not *expressly* delegated to the United States in congress assembled." The want of such a right involves no doubt a striking absurdity, but we are reduced to the dilemma either of supposing that deficiency, preposterous as it may seem, or of contravening or explaining away a provision, . . . If we are unwilling to impair the force of this applauded provision, we shall be obliged to conclude, that the United States afford the extraordinary spectacle of a government, destitute even of the shadow of constitutional power to enforce the execution of its own laws.

Document 5

Source: The Address and Reasons of Dissent of the Minority of the Convention of the State of Pennsylvania to their Constituents. December 18, 1787, *Pennsylvania Packet*

The Continental convention met in the city of Philadelphia at the time appointed. It was composed of some men of excellent characters; of others who were more remarkable for their ambition and cunning, than their patriotism; and of some who had been opponents to the independence of the United States.

* * *

Whilst the gilded chains were forging in the secret conclave, the meaner instruments of despotism without, were busily employed in alarming the fears of the people with dangers which did not exist, and exciting their hopes of greater advantages from the expected plan than even the best government on earth could produce.

* * *

In this situation of affairs were the subscribers elected members of the convention of Pennsylvania. A convention called by a legislature in direct violation of their duty, and composed in part of members, who were compelled to attend for that purpose, to consider of a constitution proposed by a convention of the United States, who were not appointed for the purpose of framing a new form of government, but whose powers were expressly confined to altering and amending the present articles confederation. Therefore the members of the continental convention in proposing the plan acted as individuals, and not as deputies from Pennsylvania. The assembly who called the state convention acted as individuals, and not as the legislature of Pennsylvania; nor could they or the convention chosen on their recommendation have authority to do any act or thing, that can alter or annihilate the constitution of Pennsylvania (both of which will be done by the new constitution) nor are their proceedings in our opinion, at all binding on the people.

Document 6

Source: James Madison, House of Representatives, February 2, 1791, M. St. Clair Clarke and D.A. Hall, comp., *Legislative and Documentary History of the Bank of the United State.* (Washington, DC: Gales and Seaton, 1832), 39–40

After some general remarks on the limitations of all political power, he [Mr. Madison] took notice of the peculiar manner in which the Federal Government is limited. It is not only a general grant out of which particular powers are excepted; it is a grant of particular powers, leaving the general mass in other hands. So it had been understood by its friends and its foes; and so it was to be interpreted.

As preliminaries to a right interpretation, he laid down the following rules: An interpretation that destroys the very characteristic of the Government cannot be just. Where a meaning is clear, the consequences, whatever they may be, are to be admitted;

* * *

Reviewing the constitution with an eye to these positions, it was not possible to discover in it the power to incorporate a bank. The only clauses under which such power could be pretended, was, either

> *First.* The power to lay and collect taxes to pay the debts and provide for the common defence and general welfare; or,

> *Second.* The power to borrow money on the credit of the United States; or,

> *Third.* The powers to pass all laws necessary and proper to carry into execution those powers.

* * *

Whatever meaning this [*third*] clause may have, none can be admitted that would give an unlimited discretion to Congress. Its meaning must, according to the natural and obvious force of the terms and the context, be limited to means *necessary* to the *end*, and *incident* to the *nature*, of the specified powers.

* * *

If the power were in the constitution, the immediate exercise of it cannot be essential; if not there, the exercise of it involves the guilt of usurpation, and establishes a precedent of interpretation, levelling all the barriers which limit the powers of the General Government. . . . It appeared on the whole, he [Mr. Madison] concluded, that the power exercised by the [bank] bill was condemned by the silence of the constitution; was condemned by the rule of interpretation, arising out of the constitution; was condemned by its tendency to destroy the main characteristic of the constitution.

Document 7

Source: Thomas Jefferson to James Madison, December 28, 1794, *Papers of Thomas Jefferson* ed. John Catanzariti et al. (Princeton: Princeton University Press, 2000), 28:228–29

The denunciation of the democratic societies is one of the extraordinary acts of boldness of which we have seen so many from the faction of Monocrats. It is wonderful indeed that the President should have permitted himself to be the organ of such an attack on the freedom of discussion, the freedom of writing, printing and publishing. It must be a matter of rare curiosity to get at the modification of these rights. . . and to see what line their ingenuity would draw between democratical societies, whose avowed object is the nourishment of the republican principles of our constitution. . . The very persons denouncing the democrats are themselves the . . . high officers. Their sight must be perfectly dazzled by the glittering of crowns and coronets, not to see the extravagance of the proposition to suppress the friends of general freedom, while those who wish to confine that freedom to the few are permitted to go on in their principles and practices.—I here put out of sight the persons whose misbehavior has been taken advantage of to slander the friends of popular rights; and I am happy to observe that as far as the circle of my observation and information extends, every body has lost sight of them, and viewed the abstract attempt on their natural and constitutional rights in all it's nakedness. I have never heard . . . a single expression or opinion which did not condemn it as an inexcusable aggression.

END OF DOCUMENTS FOR QUESTION 1

Question 2, 3, or 4 (Long Essay Question)
Suggested writing time: 40 minutes

Directions: Answer Question 2 or Question 3 or Question 4.

In your response you should do the following.

- Respond to the prompt with a historically defensible thesis or claim that establishes a line of reasoning.

- Describe a broader historical context relevant to the prompt.

- Support an argument in response to the prompt using specific and relevant examples evidence.

- Use historical reasoning (e.g., comparison, causation, continuity, or change over time) to frame or structure an argument that addresses the prompt.

- Use evidence to corroborate, qualify, or modify an argument that addresses the prompt.

2. **Evaluate the extent to which religion (religious fervor) fostered change in American society between 1730 and 1770.**

3. **Evaluate the extent to which religion (religious fervor) fostered change in American society between 1800 and 1850.**

4. **Evaluate the extent to which religion (religious fervor) fostered change in American society between 1970 and 1990.**

Practice Exam 2
SECTION I, PART A
Time—55 minutes
55 Questions

Directions: Each of the questions or incomplete statements is followed by four suggested answers or completions. Select the one that is best in each case and then fill in the corresponding answer on the answer sheet provided.

Questions 1 and 2 refer to the following excerpt.

"Spanola is a marvel; the mountains and hills, and plains, and fields . . . rich for planting and sowing, for breeding cattle . . . for building towns and villages.

"I gave [to the people of the island] . . . a thousand useful things that I carried, in order that they may conceive affection, . . . and may be made Christians. . . . [T]hey strive . . . in giving us things which they have in abundance. . . . [T]hey received me at every place where I landed, after they lost their terror. . . .

"[T]hey are men of very subtle wit. . . . I took some of them by force to the intent that they should learn [our language]. . . .

"I saw not much diversity in the looks of the people, nor in their manners and language, but they all understand each other. . . ."

> The Spanish Letter of Columbus to Luis Sant'Angel, February 15, 1493, in the
> *Personal Narrative of the First Voyage of Columbus to America*

1. Christopher Columbus's initial observations of the lands he explored in 1492–93 were that

    (A) the lands should be exploited and stripped of resources for the economic advantage of Spain

    (B) the lands had great potential to benefit European interests

    (C) Spanish officials of the king and queen should be sent to the lands to govern them effectively

    (D) he had discovered vast continents that no Europeans had ever known existed

2. Columbus's observations of the Native people he encountered included which of the following?

    (A) They were racially and culturally inferior and should be enslaved to serve Spanish landlords.

    (B) They were threats to him and to others who would follow him into the new lands.

    (C) They were culturally inferior, but there were things they had and ways they lived that could be useful to Europeans.

    (D) The diversity of their cultures and races were great and difficult for Europeans to understand.

Questions 3–5 refer to the following image.

TO BE SOLD on Thursday next, at publick vendue,
TEN LIKELY GOLD COAST NEW NEGROES,
Just imported from the West-Indies,
Consisting of eight stout men and two women.
To prevent their receiving the infection of the smallpox, they have been kept constantly on board the vessel since they arrived, where they will be sold.—Any person inclining to purchase them at private sale may apply to Messrs. Johnson and Wylly.

RUN AWAY from the subscriber, a NEGROE MAN named FRANK, who carried off a gun and shot pouch with him. He is a likely well made stout fellow, speaks broken English, with the Spanish accent, having been several years at the Havana.—Whoever will deliver him to Mr. George Baillie in Savannah, or to me in Augusta, shall receive 20s. reward, besides all charges. JAMES GRAY.

Slave auction and fugitive slave advertisements, *Georgia Gazette*, October 25, 1764, courtesy Latin American Studies,www.latinamericanstudies.org.

3. What was a major point that could be understood about the sale of slaves in the first advertisement above?

   (A) These slaves had not been exposed to smallpox so they would be a good investment.

   (B) It was more profitable to sell slaves at public auctions rather than through private sales.

   (C) There was no real market for female slaves in the 1760s.

   (D) Slaves purchased directly from Africa were usually the best bargain.

4. The slaves in both advertisements came to Georgia from the Caribbean. How did that information fit into the traditional triangular trade in slaves in the 1700s?

   (A) Slave dealers who came to the North American colonies were not allowed to come directly from Africa.

   (B) Slaves went to the Caribbean to learn to cultivate cotton.

   (C) The slaves may have been sent from Africa to the Indies and undergone the "seasoning process" there before being sold into the North American colonies.

   (D) Purchasers wanted slaves from the Caribbean because most had adopted Catholicism while enslaved there, making them less rebellious.

5. What did the description on the runaway man in the second document indicate about his resourcefulness?

    (A) He had not been a slave very long, because he still believed he might successfully escape.

    (B) Though a slave, he has learned both some Spanish and English, and he knows how to use firearms.

    (C) Slave holders had little hope of ever recapturing a runaway, because there was little incentive for people to help recover the fugitives.

    (D) This man was escaping to rejoin his family in a nearby town.

Questions 6–8 refer to the following excerpt.

"Be it enacted by the Senate and House of Representatives of the United States of America, in Congress assembled, That any person who shall appropriate, excavate, injure, or destroy any historic or prehistoric ruin or monument, or any object of antiquity, situated on lands owned or controlled by the Government of the United States . . . shall, upon conviction, be fined in a sum of not more than five hundred dollars or be imprisoned for a period of not more than ninety days, or shall suffer both fine and imprisonment, the discretion of the court. (U.S.C., title 16, sec. 433.)

"SEC 2. That the President of the United States is hereby authorized, in his discretion, to declare by public proclamation historic landmarks, historic and prehistoric structures, and other objects of historic or scientific interest that are situated upon the lands owned or controlled by the Government of the United States to be national monuments, and may reserve as a part thereof parcels of land . . . : Provided, That when such objects are situated upon tract covered by a bona fide unperfected claim or held in private ownership, the tracts . . . may be relinquished to the Government, and the Secretary of the Interior is hereby authorized to accept the relinquishment of such tracts in behalf of the Government of the United States." (U.S.C., title 16, sec. 431.)

An Act for the Preservation of American Antiquities, Approved June 8, 1906 (34 Stat. 225)

6.   How was the Antiquities Act a good example of the sort of legislation supported by Progressives at the beginning of the twentieth century?

   (A)   Progressives had little regard for private property and felt the government could take it over whenever they felt it was necessary.

   (B)   Progressives felt it was appropriate for the government to take a more active role in administering and protecting national monuments and natural resources.

   (C)   Progressives were supportive of preservation measures but only in the western states where population centers were fewer and farther between.

   (D)   Progressives wanted to increase the power of the executive branch of government as a check on Congress and the Supreme Court.

7.   According to the act, what was the role of the President of the United States in the process of preserving antiquities?

   (A)   The act gave the president the power to identify places or buildings for protection as antiquities if they were on government land.

   (B)   The President could identify sites for preservation but only with the consent and support of Congress.

   (C)   The President could choose sites for protection, but the final decisions would be made by the state where the site was located.

   (D)   The President could only name sites on public land, as sites on private land were permanently off limits.

8.   How did this act represent a different approach to government involvement from other Progressive concerns for conservation programs?

   (A)   There really was very little difference in Progressive calls for preservation and conservation, as both achieved the same ends.

   (B)   Sites that were designated for conservation could never be modified.

   (C)   This Antiquities Act called for protection and no development in the sites rather than controlled use of the resources identified.

   (D)   There were penalties for violations of antiquities sites but no penalties for violations of those designated for conservation.

Questions 9–11 refer to the following excerpt.

"Our country, in the position it has given to foreigners who have made it their home, has pursued a course in relation to them, totally different from that of any other country in the world. . . .

". . . The writer believes, that since the time of the American Revolution, which gave the principles of Democratic liberty a home, those principles have never been in greater jeopardy than at the present moment. Already have foreigners increased in the country to such a degree, that they justly give us alarm. . . .

"That they are men who having professed to become Americans, by accepting our terms of naturalization, do yet, in direct contradiction to their professions, clan together as a separate interest . . . is it not time, high time, that a true American spirit were roused to resist this alarming inroad of foreign influence upon our institutions, to avert dangers to which we have hitherto shut our eyes, and which if not remedied, and that immediately, will inevitably change the whole character of our government. I repeat what I first said, this is no party question, it concerns native Americans of all parties."

Samuel F. B. Morse, Imminent Dangers to the Free Institutions of the United States, 1835

9. The concerns expressed in the above passage foreshadowed which of the following?

    (A) Increasing fear of communist and anarchist infiltration into the U.S. political system

    (B) Rapidly increasing immigration from Southern and Eastern Europe

    (C) The influx of Irish and German Catholic immigrants

    (D) The threat to the institution of slavery posed by agricultural mechanization

10. Concerns by native-born Americans similar to those expressed by the above passage led most directly to which of the following before the Civil War?

    (A) The exclusion of Asian immigrants attempting to enter the United States

    (B) A Red Scare that infringed on the constitutional guarantees of free speech

    (C) Increased nativist sentiment resulting in the formation of a third political party

    (D) A system that established immigration quotas from individual foreign countries

11. Which of the following best describes a fundamental shift in the character of immigration by the end of the nineteenth century?

    (A) Immigrants from the Western Hemisphere greatly outnumbered those arriving from Europe

    (B) U.S. law limited immigration to skilled craftsmen needed in the industrial economy

    (C) The vast majority of immigrants during the period settled on the Great Plains

    (D) The volume of immigrants entering the United States increased dramatically

Questions 12–14 refer to the following excerpt.

"For over 40 years, the United States led the West in the struggle against Communism and the threat it posed to our most precious values.

"That confrontation is now over. The nuclear threat—while far from gone—is receding. Eastern Europe is free. The Soviet Union is no more. This is a victory for democracy and freedom. It's a victory for the moral forces of our values. Every American can take pride in this victory. . . .

"These dramatic events come at a time when Americans are facing challenges here at home.

"And I want all Americans to know that I am committed to attacking economic problems at home. . . . I am confident we will meet this challenge as we have so many times before. But we cannot if we retreat into isolationism. We will only succeed in this interconnected world by continuing to lead the fight for free people and free and fair trade. A free and prosperous global economy is essential for American prosperity."

President George H. W. Bush, *The New York Times*, December 26, 1991

12. In this speech in December 1991, President George H. W. Bush declared that

    (A) the United States and the Soviet Union had agreed to disarm all nuclear weapons

    (B) communism was no longer a threat to the United States

    (C) the Cold War was ended

    (D) the United States and the Soviet Union were joining together in an alliance to maintain peace in the world

13. President Bush suggested that in the years after 1991, the United States should

    (A) no longer play the role of policeman for world peace

    (B) pursue a foreign policy of isolationism

    (C) declare tariffs on foreign trade goods in order to strengthen the U.S. economy at home

    (D) cooperate with other nations in pursuing economic stability and world peace

14. During the 1990s, the United States did which of the following?

    (A) Faced threats from a variety of places and from people who were often more difficult to identify than the communists had been

    (B) Reduced the size of its military and avoided interactions with other nations

    (C) Conducted a military invasion of Saudi Arabia and Iran when they threatened to cut off the trade of their oil supply to the United States

    (D) Led the move to disband the United Nations

Questions 15–17 refer to the following excerpt.

"The English who came first to this country were but an handful of people, forlorn, poor and distressed. My father was then sachem [chief]. He relieved their distresses in the most kind and hospitable manner. He gave them land to build and plant upon. He did all in his power to serve them. Others of their country men came and joined them.

"My father was also the father of the English. He represented to his counselors and warriors that the English knew many sciences which the Indians did not; that they improved and cultivated the earth, and raised cattle and fruits, and that there was sufficient room in the country for both the English and the Indians. His advise prevailed. It was concluded to give victuals to the English. . . .

"By various means they got possessed of a great part of his territory. But he still remained their friend until he died. My elder brother became sachem. They pretended to suspect him of evil designs against them. He was seized and confined, and thereby thrown into sickness and died. Soon after I became sachem they disarmed all my people. They tried my people by their own laws and assessed damages against them which they could not pay. Their land was taken.

"Sometimes the cattle of the English would come into the cornfields of my people, for they did not make fences like the English. I must then be seized and confined till I sold another tract of my country for satisfaction of all damages and costs. But a small part of the dominion of my ancestors remains. I am determined not to live till I have no country."

King Philip, 1676.

15. King Philip's account of troubles between English settlers and American Indians highlighted which of the following, among other things?

   (A) English and American Indian hostilities were not a foregone conclusion at the time of English settlement.

   (B) European diseases had almost immediately decimated native populations in New England.

   (C) Native tribes felt shortchanged by the purchase prices offered by English settlers.

   (D) American Indian livestock destroyed the crops of English farmers, leading to increased hostilities.

16. Prior to the French and Indian War, New England settlers and American Indians

   (A) invaded and captured French Canada

   (B) engaged in serious military confrontations with each other

   (C) formed the New England Confederation to protect against French attacks

   (D) had little direct contact with each other

17. According to the above passage, the primary cause of conflict between New England colonists and American Indians was

   (A) colonists' encroachment on Indian lands

   (B) the farming practices of Native Americans

   (C) exclusion of American Indians from the lucrative fur trade

   (D) colonial overfishing of the waters off the New England coast

Questions 18–20 refer to the following image.

Protest on Behalf of a Fugitive Slave Citizens of Boston! A Free Citizen of Massachusetts—Free by Massachusetts Laws until His Liberty is Declared to be Forfeited by a Massachusetts Jury, is Now Imprisoned . . . Boston: s.n., ca. 1855. Samuel J. May Anti-Slavery Collection

18. What federal action led to the events surrounding this 1855 Boston poster?

   (A)   The Kansas-Nebraska Act

   (B)   The Compromise of 1850

   (C)   The *Dred Scott v. Sanford* decision

   (D)   The Treaty of Guadalupe-Hidalgo

19. Why did the creator of this poster remind the people of Boston that they were the "sons of Otis, and Hancock, and the 'Brace of Adamses'"?

   (A)   Those men had been arrested earlier for kidnapping runaway slaves.

   (B)   Massachusetts was the birthplace of the American Revolution, led by patriots who also opposed slavery.

   (C)   Otis, Hancock, and the Adamses were strong supporters of the Underground Railroad.

   (D)   All three of these men wanted Massachusetts to leave the Union if slavery continued to be legal.

20. Actions like those called for in this poster were an example of which of the following?

    (A) Nullification

    (B) Nativism

    (C) Anarchy

    (D) Utopianism

Questions 21–23 refer to the following excerpt.

"When the strongest nation in the world can be tied down for four years in a war in Vietnam with no end in sight; when the richest nation in the world can't manage its own economy; when the nation with the greatest tradition of the rule of law is plagued by unprecedented lawlessness; when a nation that has been known for a century for equality of opportunity is torn by unprecedented racial violence; and when the President of the United States cannot travel abroad or to any major city at home without fear of a hostile demonstration—then it's time for new leadership for the United States of America."

Richard Nixon, Acceptance Speech at the Republican National Convention, August 8, 1968

21. The above appeal to the American people was aimed primarily at winning the votes of

(A) college students whose numbers had increased significantly as a result of the baby boom

(B) blue-collar workers who were disenchanted with protest movements and civil unrest

(C) African American voters whose numbers had increased as a result of the Voting Rights Act of 1965

(D) women's rights advocates who were pushing for an equal rights amendment to the Constitution

22. Nixon's victory in the election of 1968 signaled which of the following trends in U.S. political history?

(A) Movement from the conservative philosophy of Democratic administrations to a more liberal ideology

(B) Rejection of the social welfare state, Social Security, and federally mandated minimum wages

(C) The breakup of the traditional stronghold of Democrats in the American South

(D) The realignment of African American voters from the Democratic Party to the Republican Party

23. Nixon's victory in 1968 was, in part, the direct result of

(A) the Democratic Party's abandonment of liberal principles embodied in the New Deal and Great Society.

(B) disarray within the Democratic Party as evidenced by the Democratic national convention

(C) the failure to oust communist dictatorships in the Caribbean

(D) his guarantee of a national health insurance program for the American people

Questions 24–26 refer to the following excerpt.

"In the beginning, God ordained that man should labor, not as a curse, but as a blessing; not as a punishment, but as means of development, physically, mentally, morally, and has set thereunto his seal of approval in the rich increase and reward. By labor is brought forward the kindly fruits of the earth in rich abundance for our sustenance and comfort; by labor (not exhaustive) is promoted health of the body and strength of mind, labor garners the priceless stores of wisdom and knowledge. It is the 'Philosopher's Stone,' everything it touches turns to wealth. 'Labor is noble and holy.' To glorify God in its exercise, to defend it from degradation, to divest it of the evils to body, mind, and estate, which ignorance and greed have imposed; to rescue the toiler from the grasp of the selfish is a work worthy of the noblest and best of our race.

"You have been selected from among your associates for that exalted purpose. Are you willing to accept the responsibility, and, trusting in the support of pledged true Knights, labor, with what ability you possess, for the triumph of these principles among men?"

Adelphon Kruptos, The Secret Work of the Knights of Labor, 1869

24. Which of the following was true of the Knights of Labor?

    (A) They organized only skilled workers.

    (B) They favored violent confrontation with big business to achieve their goals.

    (C) They experienced greater success than any subsequent labor union.

    (D) They were organized into one big union of both skilled and unskilled workers.

25. To what extent were the Knights of Labor successful in improving the lives of workers?

    (A) They secured federal minimum wage and maximum hour laws by 1900.

    (B) They were largely unsuccessful in combating the power of big business during the time period.

    (C) By 1900 they had emerged as the leading labor union in the United States.

    (D) Their violent tactics of murder and arson weakened their status in the minds of the public.

26. The American Federation of Labor differed from the Knights of Labor in that

    (A) it had a greater focus on bread-and-butter unionism

    (B) it abandoned the strike as a tool in labor disputes

    (C) it included African Americans and women within its ranks

    (D) it formed a staunch alliance with the Republican Party

Questions 27–29 refer to the following excerpt.

"It is proposed that humble application be made for an act of Parliament of Great Britain, by virtue of which one general government may be formed in America including all the said colonies . . .

1. That said general government be administered by a president-General, to be appointed and supported by the crown. . . .

2. That . . . the House of Representatives . . . shall choose members for a Grand Council in the following proportions [representatives of each state. . . .

3. That there shall be a new election of the members of the Grand Council every three years. . . .

11. That they make such laws as they judge necessary for regulating all Indian trade.

15. That they raise and pay soldiers and build forts for the defence of any of the Colonies. . . .

16. That for these purposes they have power to make laws, and lay and levy such general duties, imposts, or taxes, as to them shall appear most equal and just. . . .

21. That the laws made by them for the purposes aforesaid shall not be repugnant, but as near as may be, agreeable to the laws of England, and shall be transmitted to the King in Council for approbation. . . ."

Benjamin Franklin, Albany Plan of Union (1754)

27. What were the historical circumstances that led to Franklin's proposal for the Albany Plan of Union?

    (A) The American Revolution against Great Britain had just been declared.

    (B) The colonies were fighting the French and Indian War as subjects of Great Britain.

    (C) The colonies were fighting among themselves over trade with the Spanish and the Indians.

    (D) The British government had asked the colonists to assume a greater role in governing themselves in preparation for independence.

28. What was Benjamin Franklin proposing in his Albany Plan of Union?

    (A) He was proposing that the colonies renounce their allegiance to Great Britain and declare independence.

    (B) He was urging colonists to arm themselves and build forts to resist British troops .

    (C) He proposed creating a representative government while still allowing the British to have a say in who was chosen to serve in the colonial assembly.

    (D) He was proposing a limited form of self-government relying on local control with the assent and cooperation of Great Britain.

29. How did Franklin's proposal reflect the influence of the Enlightenment on his thinking?

    (A) Franklin believed in the Enlightenment principle of allowing men to have an equal say in how they were to be governed.

    (B) He believed in the concept of a representative government if the people were able to obtain the monarch's permission.

    (C) He supported the idea that taxation and tariffs should be made in consultation with the monarch.

    (D) He did not advocate the creation of a military, as he believed all men should be governed by reason and natural rights.

Questions 30–32 refer to the following excerpt.

"Fourscore and seven years ago our fathers brought forth, on this continent, a new nation, conceived in liberty, and dedicated to the proposition that all men are created equal. Now we are engaged in a great civil war, testing whether that nation, or any nation so conceived, and so dedicated, can long endure. We are met on a great battle-field of that war. We have come to dedicate a portion of that field, as a final resting-place for those who here gave their lives, that that nation might live. It is altogether fitting and proper that we should do this. But, in a larger sense, we cannot dedicate, we cannot consecrate—we cannot hallow—this ground. The brave men, living and dead, who struggled here, have consecrated it far above our poor power to add or detract. The world will little note, nor long remember what we say here, but it can never forget what they did here. It is for us the living, rather, to be dedicated here to the unfinished work which they who fought here have thus far so nobly advanced. It is rather for us to be here dedicated to the great task remaining before us—that from these honored dead we take increased devotion to that cause for which they here gave the last full measure of devotion—that we here highly resolve that these dead shall not have died in vain—that this nation, under God, shall have a new birth of freedom, and that government of the people, by the people, for the people, shall not perish from the earth."

Abraham Lincoln, "Gettysburg Address," November 19, 1863

30. What was Lincoln's primary purpose in the Gettysburg Address?

   (A) He wanted to be sure that all Americans understood the need for organizing cemeteries for the war dead.

   (B) He was celebrating the victorious conclusion of the Civil War.

   (C) He wanted people to see the Civil War as being about more than simply keeping the Union together.

   (D) He hoped to make people realize that democracy in the United States had never been threatened by the war.

31. From what document foundational to the creation of the United States did he quote the phrase ". . . all men are created equal"?

   (A) The United States Constitution

   (B) The Bill of Rights

   (C) The Declaration of Independence

   (D) The Federalist Papers

32. This address was seen as a call for support of what major goal of Lincoln's presidency?

   (A) Equal rights for women

   (B) The end of slavery

   (C) Better treatment of veterans

   (D) Rededication to church membership and support

Questions 33–35 refer to the following map

The Great Migration, 1916–1930

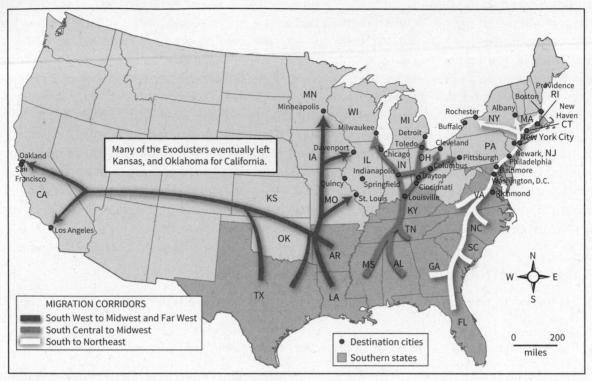

Many of the Exodusters eventually left Kansas, and Oklahoma for California.

MIGRATION CORRIDORS
South West to Midwest and Far West
South Central to Midwest
South to Northeast

● Destination cities
▪ Southern states

Map by Michael Siegel Rutgers Cartography 2005
Source: "The Atlas of African-American History and Politics"

33. What accounted for such large numbers of African Americans leaving the South between 1916 and 1930?

   (A) The legacy of Jim Crow along with the rebirth of the Ku Klux Klan and the hardships of sharecropping led many to make the decision to leave.

   (B) Many southern landowners encouraged African Americans to leave because they wanted to bring in cheaper Mexican laborers.

   (C) The newly formed NAACP actively recruited southern farm workers to go North to take better-paying factory jobs.

   (D) Southern farm workers were paid bonuses by Northern and midwestern industries that hoped to lure them to factory work.

34. How did World War I play a role in accelerating the migration shown in the map above?

    (A) The government issued a military draft for all men, whether they were minorities or not, as the Armed Forces were newly desegregated.

    (B) African American men were called to provide defense forces along the northern coast to protect American munitions facilities.

    (C) World War I took many men out of the northern and midwestern job markets and opened opportunities for the migrants.

    (D) African American sharecroppers were recruited to grain-producing states in the North and Midwest to help supply the troops with food.

35. Which of the following was a common experience of the thousands who decided to relocate to cities outside of the South?

    (A) Few had any regrets because they found they got pay and benefits equal to that of white workers.

    (B) Though job opportunities were often better, many still encountered racism and discrimination in other parts of the country.

    (C) Most completely forgot the cultural traditions and connections with the South as they worked to become a part of their new communities.

    (D) Few stayed more than a few years, and by the 1940s the migration trend had reversed with most returning to their previous homes.

Questions 36–38 refer to the following image.

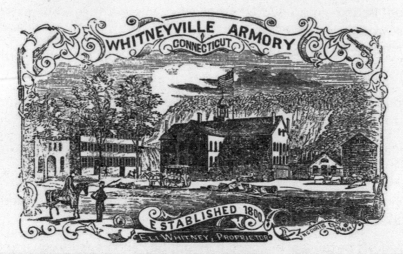

Library of Congress, Prints & Photographs Division, Reproduction number HAER CONN,5-HAM,3--21

36. Eli Whitney's major contribution to the first Industrial Revolution in the United States centered around

    (A) the development of interchangeable parts

    (B) transportation innovations that allowed travel upriver

    (C) agricultural innovations that led to higher grain production

    (D) development of the American System, which linked all sections of the country together economically

37. Which of the following was true of the first Industrial Revolution in the United States?

    (A) Slaves were the dominant source of labor in New England textile mills.

    (B) New England farm girls provided a significant source of labor.

    (C) Southern and Eastern European immigrants made up majority of New England factory workers.

    (D) Federal law prevented Irish immigrants from working in American industry.

38. Which of the following factors provided the greatest impetus for initial industrial development in the United States?

    (A) European demand for American industrial products

    (B) Vast deposits of iron ore and coal in New England

    (C) Technological revolutions in both transportation and agriculture

    (D) Extensive federal government subsidies for the development of manufacturing

Questions 39–41 refer to the following excerpt.

"The contrast between the palace of the millionaire and the cottage of the laborer with us today measures the change which has come with civilization. This change, however, is not to be deplored, but welcomed as highly beneficial. . . .

"We accept and welcome therefore, as conditions to which we must accommodate ourselves, great inequality of environment, the concentration of business, industrial and commercial, in the hands of a few, and the law of competition between these, as being not only beneficial, but essential for the future progress of the race.

"This, then, is held to be the duty of the man of Wealth: First, to set an example of modest, unostentatious living, shunning display or extravagance; to provide moderately for the legitimate wants of those dependent upon him; and after doing so to consider all surplus revenues which come to him simply as trust funds, which he is called upon to administer, and strictly bound as a matter of duty to administer in the manner which, in his judgment, is best calculated to produce the most beneficial results for the community—the man of wealth thus becoming the mere agent and trustee for his poorer brethren, bringing to their service his superior wisdom, experience and ability to administer, doing for them better than they would or could do for themselves.

"'The man who dies thus rich dies disgraced.'"

Andrew Carnegie, The Gospel of Wealth, 1889

39. The above passage fits most closely with which of the following philosophies prevalent in the time period?

    (A) Anarchy, which held that all governments needed to be overthrown

    (B) Socialism, which saw the government as the protector of social welfare

    (C) Social Darwinism, which held that the fittest in society naturally prevailed

    (D) Pragmatism, which held that utility was the ultimate determiner of truth

40. Carnegie demonstrated opposition to which of the following?

    (A) The formation of monopolies

    (B) Accumulation of wealth in the hands of the few

    (C) Conspicuous consumption by the wealthy

    (D) Horizontal and vertical integration of business

41. Carnegie believed which of the following?

    (A) Those chosen to amass great fortunes knew the best way to help the poor.

    (B) Equality of income should become a guiding principle in American life.

    (C) The poor chose to be poor and deserved no help.

    (D) Excess wealth should be turned over to the federal government for redistribution.

Questions 42–44 refer to the following image.

Library of Congress, Prints & Photographs Division, Reproduction number LC-DIG-ppmsc-03479

42. The political cartoon above best reflected which of the following?

 (A) Corruption associated with the Gilded Age

 (B) Abuse of presidential power made public in the 1970s, which led to impeachment proceedings

 (C) Hysteria over the fear of communist infiltration into the U.S. government

 (D) Revelations concerning war crimes during the war in Vietnam

43. The ultimate result of the events depicted in the cartoon resulted in

 (A) the resignation of a president

 (B) the end of boss rule in New York City

 (C) the discrediting of a U.S. Senator

 (D) prison terms for cabinet members

44. During national emergencies, which of the following tends to be true?

    (A) Civil liberties are constricted through espionage and sedition acts.

    (B) The federal government gives up power to the states.

    (C) Federal courts rigidly defend First Amendment rights.

    (D) The executive branch gives up power to the legislative branch.

Questions 45–47 refer to the following image.

April 4, 1891, Where the Blame Lies. Judge (to Uncle Sam)—"If Immigration was properly Restricted you would no longer be troubled with Anarchy, Socialism, the Mafia, and such kindred evils!"

Louis Dalrymple, "The High Tide of Immigration—A National Menace," *Judge Magazine*, August 22, 1903. Library of Congress, Prints & Photographs Division, Reproduction number LC-USZC4-5739

45. What events in the early twentieth century led Americans to be concerned about a possible influx of immigrants into the United States?

(A) American industrialists were advertising in Europe and Far East for more workers to keep their factories busy.

(B) The United States had acquired overseas possessions, and many Americans worried that this would lead to massive waves of immigration to the United States.

(C) Word had reached other parts of the world that the United States government had passed laws preventing nativist discrimination, making immigration more appealing.

(D) The United States had decided to offer help with housing and health care for immigrants who needed it, thus leading to a drastic increase in immigrants

46. Who in the United States was most worried about this possible mass migration?

    (A) Major industrialists feared increased difficulty hiring workers as many of the new arrivals would not speak English and would have no industrial skills.

    (B) Many workers feared losing jobs; others complained that these immigrants would create racial and religious tensions.

    (C) Those living in the West were afraid new immigrants would rush to buy homesteads and drive up the costs of land.

    (D) The United States military was concerned about being able to protect American borders if immigration numbers became too large.

47. How did the United States government address these fears two decades later in the 1920s?

    (A) Congress enacted a series of laws offering financial support and language training to help newly arriving immigrants adjust to American life more quickly.

    (B) Immigrants were still allowed to enter the United States but only if they already had family here and could demonstrate job skills and literacy.

    (C) Immigration from Asia was halted completely, while the numbers allowed in from other parts of the world were not affected.

    (D) Congress passed two immigration quota acts that drastically reduced the number of people eligible to immigrate to the United States.

Questions 48–50 refer to the following excerpt.

"One of the most interesting events of the past week, was the holding of what is technically styled a Woman's Rights Convention at Seneca Falls. . . . Several interesting documents setting forth the rights as well as the grievances of women were read. Among these was a declaration of sentiments, to be regarded as the basis of a grand movement for attaining all the civil, social, political and religious rights of women. . . . Many who have at last made the discovery that negroes had some rights as well as other members of the human family, have yet to be convinced that woman is entitled to any . . . a number of persons of this description actually abandoned the anti-slavery cause . . . lest . . . they might possibly be giving countenance the dangerous heresy that woman . . . stands on an equal footing with man. . . .

"We are free to say that . . . we hold woman to be justly entitled to all we claim for man. . . . All that distinguished man as an intelligent and accountable human being, is equally true of woman; and if that government is only just which governs by the free consent of the governed, there can be no reason in the world for denying to woman the exercise of the elective franchise, or a hand in making and administering the laws of the land. . . . We therefore bid the women engaged in this movement our humble God-speed."

Frederick Douglass, "The Rights of Women," *The North Star*, July 28, 1848

48. What was Frederick Douglass's opinion of the Seneca Falls Convention that met in New York in 1848?

(A) Douglass felt women should have equal social and religious rights, but he was unsure about political rights.

(B) He was a full supporter of women's rights and committed to ending slavery.

(C) He believed that the abolition of slavery should occur before women's suffrage.

(D) Douglass wanted the women at Seneca Falls to know that all abolitionists wholeheartedly supported their cause.

49. What point did Douglass make about the connection between the abolitionist movement and the movement to secure equal rights for women?

(A) He argued that women hindered the abolitionist movement by speaking at public gatherings.

(B) He was confident that abolitionist groups would be united in their support for equal rights for women.

(C) He felt that most abolitionists saw the issue of women's rights as completely separate from abolition, so there was no conflict between the two.

(D) He admitted that some people had abandoned the abolitionist cause to avoid having to also support women's rights.

50. When Douglass spoke of a government "which governs by the consent of the governed," he was drawing on the ideals of which of the following?

(A) The Enlightenment

(B) Transcendentalism

(C) Federalism

(D) Romanticism

Questions 51–53 refer to the following image.

GETTING TROUBLESOME AGAIN.

UNCLE SAM.—I guess he won't stop howling till I give him enough Protection Soothing Syrup to burst him!

Getting Troublesome Again. Uncle Sam—I guess he won't stop howling till I give him enough Protection Soothing Syrup to burst him!

GRANGER

51. Which of the following reflects the artist's point of view in the political cartoon shown above?

(A) The American infant industry needed a competitive advantage from foreign competitors.

(B) American industry had outgrown its need for high protective tariffs.

(C) It was not the federal government's duty to look after the needs of big business.

(D) The federal government should pursue a laissez-faire policy toward business regulation.

52. During the Gilded Age, the federal government was increasingly seen as

    (A) far too engaged in the overregulation of big business

    (B) unwilling to protect American industry from foreign competition

    (C) unconcerned about the preservation of the environment

    (D) a resource to correct the real and perceived abuses of big business

53. Which of the following was true concerning the federal government during the late nineteenth century?

    (A) It took initial steps toward the regulation of big business.

    (B) It tended to side with organized labor in disputes with big business.

    (C) It enacted significant social welfare legislation to protect disadvantaged groups.

    (D) The income tax became the chief source of revenue for the federal government

Questions 54 and 55 refer to the following excerpt.

"[Our taxes have] not kept pace with public spending. For decades, we have piled deficit upon deficit, mortgaging out future and our children's future. . . .

"We must act today to preserve tomorrow.

"Well, this administration's objective will be a healthy, vigorous, growing economy that provides equal opportunity for all Americans, with no barriers born of bigotry or discrimination. Putting America back to work means putting all Americans back to work. Ending inflation means freeing all Americans from the terror of runaway living costs. All must share in the productive work of this 'new beginning' and all must share in the bounty of a revived economy. With the idealism and fair play which are the core of our system and our strength, we can have a strong and prosperous American at peace with itself and the world."

President Ronald Reagan, First Inaugural Address, January 20, 1981

54. In order to accomplish what President Ronald Reagan talked about in his first inaugural address,

    (A) government spending programs like Social Security and Medicaid were permanently terminated

    (B) the government saved money by spending less on military equipment

    (C) the national government imposed a wide variety of regulations on private businesses

    (D) taxes for the wealthiest Americans in the United States were reduced

55. As a leader of the growing conservative movement in the United States, President Reagan

    (A) worked for a more limited role for the national government of the United States in the economy and in the activities of businesses

    (B) pursued a policy of isolationism and noninvolvement in foreign affairs in order to save money and to reduce the size of the government's debts

    (C) pursued an aggressive government policy to insure the civil rights of African Americans and equal rights for the LGBT communities

    (D) increased government programs that created free government housing for America's homeless citizens

CHAPTER FOUR : PRACTICE EXAMS 1 AND 2

AT THIS POINT ON THE ACTUAL EXAM,
YOU WOULD BE ALLOWED TO CHECK WORK
ON PART A, BUT NOT CONTINUE ON TO PART B.

Multiple-Choice Answer Sheet

1. _____
2. _____
3. _____
4. _____
5. _____
6. _____
7. _____
8. _____
9. _____
10. _____
11. _____
12. _____
13. _____
14. _____
15. _____
16. _____
17. _____
18. _____
19. _____

20. _____
21. _____
22. _____
23. _____
24. _____
25. _____
26. _____
27. _____
28. _____
29. _____
30. _____
31. _____
32. _____
33. _____
34. _____
35. _____
36. _____
37. _____
38. _____

39. _____
40. _____
41. _____
42. _____
43. _____
44. _____
45. _____
46. _____
47. _____
48. _____
49. _____
50. _____
51. _____
52. _____
53. _____
54. _____
55. _____

PRACTICE EXAM 2
SECTION I, PART B
Time—40 minutes

Directions: Answer Question 1 **and** Question 2. Answer **either** Question 3 **or** Question 4.

Write your response to each question on the lined page designated for that response. Each response is expected to fit within the space provided.

In your responses, be sure to address all parts of the questions you answer. Use complete sentences; an outline or bulleted list alone is not acceptable. You should write your answers on the appropriate blank answer sheets provided below. **Note: No credit will be given on the exam for responses in the wrong location.**

Short-Answer Question 1

"[Reconstruction produced] years of revolutionary turmoil. . . . The prevailing note was one of tragedy.[. . .] Never have American public men in responsible positions directing the destiny of the nation, been so brutal, hypocritical, and corrupt.

"[T]he real significance of the revolutionary proceedings of the rugged conspirators working out the policies of Thaddeus Stevens [created for] the Southern people . . . the indignities to which they were subjected. [. . .] Brutal men, inspired by personal ambition or party motives assumed the pose of philanthropists and patriots and thus deceived and misguided vast numbers of well-meaning people in the North."

Claude G. Bowers, *The Tragic Era: The Revolution after Lincoln*, 1929

"Uniting [Thaddeus] Stevens, [Charles] Sumner, and the other Radicals in 1865 was the conviction that the Civil War constituted a 'golden moment' for far-reaching change. The driving force of Radical ideology was the utopian vision of a nation whose citizens enjoyed equality of civil and political rights secured by a powerful and beneficent national state.

"[T]he Radicals embraced the wartime expansion of national authority, determined not to allow federalism and states' rights to obstruct a sweeping national effort to define and protect the rights of citizens."

Eric Foner, *A Short History of Reconstruction, 1863–1877*, 1990

1. Using the excerpts above, answer (a), (b), and (c).

   a) Briefly describe ONE major difference between Bowers's and Foner's historical interpretations of the leaders of Reconstruction after the Civil War.

   b) Briefly describe ONE specific event or development not mentioned in the document that could be used to support Foner's argument in the second excerpt.

   c) Briefly describe how both Bowers and Foner see Reconstruction as producing revolutionary or significant change in the United States after the Civil War.

Short-Answer Question 2

"[T]he manner in which other nations have undertaken to intrude themselves into [Texas] . . . in a spirit of hostile interference against us, for the avowed object of thwarting our policy and hampering our power, limiting our greatness and checking the fulfillment of our manifest destiny to overspread the continent allotted by Providence for the free development of our yearly multiplying millions."

> John L. O'Sullivan, "Annexation," *The United States Magazine and Democratic Review*, 1845

2. Using the excerpt above, answer (a), (b), and (c).

  a) Briefly explain what John L. O'Sullivan means by "manifest destiny" as expressed in the excerpt.

  b) Briefly describe ONE cause for O'Sullivan's call for manifest destiny.

  c) Briefly describe ONE specific result of manifest destiny.

Question 3 or 4

Directions: Answer **either** Question 3 **or** Question 4.

Short-Answer Question 3

3. Answer (a), (b), and (c).

  a) Briefly explain how the ideals and goals of the American Revolution led some to question the existence of slavery in the newly independent states.

  b) Briefly describe ONE specific action taken after the Revolution that reduced the number of slaves in the newly independent states.

  c) Briefly describe ONE specific reason why the number of slaves began to increase by 1800.

Short-Answer Question 4

4. Answer (a), (b), and (c).

  a) Briefly describe ONE similarity between the New Deal program of President Franklin D. Roosevelt (1933–1941) and the Great Society program of President Lyndon B. Johnson (1963–1969).

  b) Briefly explain ONE specific program or policy of the New Deal.

  c) Briefly explain ONE specific program or policy of the Great Society.

Short-Answer Response Sheets

Question 1

_____

_____

_____

_____

_____

_____

_____

_____

_____

_____

_____

_____

_____

_____

_____

_____

_____

_____

_____

_____

_____

_____

_____

_____

_____

_____

Question 2

Question 3

Question 4

SECTION II: FREE-RESPONSE QUESTIONS

Practice Exam 2
Total Time—1 hour and 40 minutes
Question 1 (Document-Based Question)
Suggested reading and writing time: 1 hour

It is suggested that you spend 15 minutes reading the documents and 45 minutes writing your response on additional paper. You will be provided an answer booklet when you take the AP examination.

Note: You may begin writing your response before the reading period is over.

Directions: Question 1 is based on the accompanying documents. The documents have been edited for the purpose of this exercise.

In your response you should do the following:

- Respond to the prompt with a historically defensible thesis or claim that establishes a line of reasoning.

- Describe a broader historical context relevant to the prompt.

- Support an argument in response to the prompt using at least six documents.

- Use at least one additional piece of specific historical evidence (beyond that found in the documents) relevant to an argument about the prompt.

- For at least three documents, explain how or why the document's point of view, purpose, historical situation, and/or audience is relevant to an argument.

- Use evidence to corroborate, qualify, or modify an argument that addresses the prompt.

1. Evaluate the extent to which American attitudes toward the proper role of the U.S. in world affairs changed in the period 1919 to 1940.

Document 1

Source: NYTribune March 7, 1920

Old Rhyme—New Reason

Who killed cock robin!
"I," said Senator Lodge;
"It was my little dodge!
I killed cock robin!"

Who saw him die?
"I," said the fly;
It does make me cry!
I saw him die!"

Who'll toll the bell?
"I," said John Bull;
'I'll give it a pull!
I'll toll the bell!"

Document 2

Source: "1917–1927," *The Nation*, April 6, 1927

"And Europe? Well, look at it. Is there any sign there that the last war is over, that the next is not on its way? Have the trustees of civilization made an arrangement under which Europe can live in peace? We doubt it. . . .The predictions and promises of 1917 are sad reading today. The United States might have led in liquidating the war had our leaders seen and understood it in the light of past history. Instead they greeted it as a "different" war, a holy crusade, prolonged it to its bitter conclusion, and made inevitable a treaty of peace as sadistic as any treaty that has disgraced the pages of recorded history. Our President and our people were betrayed by that treaty, but, unhappily, not many have realized the fact. It dashed every hope of a regenerated world, and not even the League of Nations can make much impression on the forces which it set in motion. . . .The lapse of ten years can hardly give a thrill of satisfaction to those who brought us into the war, who commemorate it with pride while handing its bleak heritage of burdens and hates to the generation coming after."

Document 3

Source: "But, Monsieur, Where Does it Bend?" TARIFF CARTOON, 1927.

"BUT, MONSIEUR, WHERE DOES IT BEND?"

GRANGER

Document 4

Source: Neutrality Act, August 31, 1935 August 31, 1935, Joint Resolution 49 stat. 1081; 22 U.S.C. 441

"Resolved by the Senate and House of Representatives of the United States of America in Congress assembled, That upon the outbreak or during the progress of war between, or among, two or more foreign states, the President shall proclaim such fact, and it shall thereafter be unlawful to export arms, ammunition, or implements of war from any place in the United States, or possessions of the United States, to any port of such belligerent states, or to any neutral port for transshipment to, or for the use of, a belligerent country.

The President, by proclamation, shall definitely enumerate the arms, ammunition, or implements of war, the export of which is prohibited by this Act.

The President may, from time to time, by proclamation, extend such embargo upon the export of arms, ammunition, or implements of war to other states as and when they may become involved in such war."

Document 5

Source: Report of the Special Committee on Investigation of the Munitions Industry (The Nye Report), U.S. Congress, Senate, 74th Congress, 2nd sess., February 24, 1936.

"The Committee finds, under the head of sales methods of the munitions companies, that almost without exception, the American munitions companies investigated have at times resorted to such unusual approaches, questionable favors and commissions, and methods of "doing the needful" as to constitute, in effect, a form of bribery of foreign governmental officials or of their close friends in order to secure business.

* * *

"The committee finds such practices on the part of any munitions company, domestic or foreign, to be highly unethical, a discredit to American business, and an unavoidable reflection upon those American governmental agencies which have unwittingly aided in the transactions so contaminated.

* * *

"The committee finds also that there is a very considerable threat to the peace and civic progress of other nations in the success of the munitions makers and of their agents in corrupting the officials of any one nation and thereby selling to that one nation an armament out of proportion to its previous armaments. Whether such extraordinary sales are procured through bribery or through other forms of salesmanship, the effect of such sales is to produce fear, hostility, and greater munitions orders on the part of neighboring countries, culminating in economic strain and collapse or war."

Document 6

Source: Secretary of State Cordell Hull, "Memorandum of Conversation with Japanese Ambassador Yoshida," June 13, 1936

"Mr. Yoshida, Japanese Ambassador to England, . . . stated that he was very desirous of promoting better relations and better understanding between our two countries. He said that the one big fact which he wanted the American people to recognize was the immense and rapidly growing population of Japan and the absolute necessity for more territory for their existence.

* * *

"In reply, I told Mr. Yoshida that I would speak frankly but in the friendliest possible spirit and say that the impression among many persons in this country was that Japan sought absolute economic domination, first of eastern Asia and then of other portions as she might see fit. . . That the upshot of the entire movement would be to exclude countries like the United States from trading with all of those portions of China thus brought under the domination or controlling influence of so-called of Japan. . . .

". . . There was no reason, in my judgment why countries like Japan, the United States, and England could not in the most amicable spirit, and with perfect justice and fairness to each, agree to assert and abide by the worldwide principle of equality in all commercial and industrial affairs."

Document 7

Source: Archibald MacLeish, *The Irresponsibles* (1940), q.v. *Annals of America* 16:2–3, 5

"The study of beauty, the study of history, the study of science, has occupied our whole hearts and the misfortunes of our generation are none of our concern. They are the practical and political concern of practical and political men but the concern of the scholar, the concern of the artist, is with other, purer, more enduring things.

* * *

"Nothing is more characteristic of the intellectuals of our generation than their failure to understand the world. . . . And yet they continue to pretend they do not know. They continue to speak of the crisis of their time as though the war in Europe, . . . they say, is no concern of theirs.

* * *

". . . We had seen, that this was not a war fought in the open on the military front, but a war fought in the back street and on the dark stair—a war fought within the city, within the house, within the mind—a war of treasons: a war of corruption: a war of lies."

END OF DOCUMENTS FOR QUESTION 1

Question 2, 3, or 4 (Long Essay Question)
Suggested writing time: 40 minutes

Directions: Answer Question 2 or Question 3 or Question 4.

In your response you should do the following:

- Respond to the prompt with a historically defensible thesis or claim that establishes a line of reasoning.

- Describe a broader historical context relevant to the prompt.

- Support an argument in response to the prompt using specific and relevant examples of evidence.

- Use historical reasoning (e.g., comparison, causation, continuity, or change over time) to frame or structure an argument that addresses the prompt.

- Use evidence to corroborate, qualify, or modify an argument that addresses the prompt.

2. **Evaluate the causes that led some of the newly independent states to question the appropriate role of the central government between 1783 and 1800.**

3. **Evaluate the causes that led the South to question the appropriate role of the central government between 1820 and 1860.**

4. **Evaluate the causes that led some Americans to question the appropriate role of the central government in protecting individual rights between 1950 and 1980.**

A Final Note

Don't Panic: Even Some History Professors Didn't Get Credit for APUSH

Tips for the Night Before and the Following Day

Don't panic! You've worked hard all year, completed our Instructional Exam, and taken and reviewed the Practice Tests; now what? It's the night before the exam, and there are so many things you don't remember: the precise vote on the Chinese Exclusion Act, what Chester Arthur died of—or for that matter who Chester Arthur was—which state's vote decided the ratification of the Constitution, who Richard Nixon's first vice-president was, and lots of other facts. The night before this or any exam you need to learn to distinguish the things you can do that will affect your performance from the things that won't. Cramming an additional fact or twenty or a hundred into your short-term memory won't matter statistically all that much. Only so many things can be put on a 3-hour 15-minute test. Nobody is expected to get a perfect score. The great theologian Reinhold Niebuhr provides the perfect wisdom for moments like these: "Grant me the serenity to accept the things I cannot change, the courage to change the things I can, and the wisdom to know the difference." What can you do at 8:00 pm the night before APUSH?

Before the Exam

- Take some quiet time to unwind and relax.

- Make sure you get a good night's sleep.

- Have a good, high-protein, low-carbohydrate breakfast. Carbs might be good for marathons, but they're not good for mental activity because they make you drowsy.

- Leave extra time to get to the exam site.

- Bring extra pens and sharpened pencils.

During the Exam

- Read the MCQ stimuli, questions, and distractors carefully. Remember to choose the best answer and beware of partially correct distractors.

- Check your answers if you have time.

- Read the SAQs, DBQ, and LEQs carefully.

- Write complete sentences when responding to the SAQs.

  - SAQs are read online; if you follow directions, it is easier for the reader to see where you score the point.

CHAPTER FIVE : A FINAL NOTE

- For all the free response questions, think, plan, and gather your thoughts even if only briefly before beginning to write.

- Write clearly, legibly, and preferably in ink.

  - Clarity in writing and organization makes it easy for readers to identify where you have satisfied the rubric.

- On the DBQ, use the 15-minute planning time to read the documents and plan and organize your essay before beginning to write.

- Budget your time: 1 hour on the DBQ and 40 minutes on the LEQs.

- Take a minute or two to select and organize your LEQs. Determine a list of facts to be included to support your argument.

Don't despair. Anything can go wrong on a single day and on a single test. It's one day. Whether you get a 1 or a 5, it is not the definitive mark of you as a student of U.S. history. It is one score on one day. As a student of history, you know that what characterizes a historical development isn't a single action or circumstance but a pattern over time. We actually know someone who took APUSH and didn't get credit yet went on to become a history professor and APUSH chief reader. The ability to think historically, reason analytically, and remember a great deal of history doesn't occur in a week, a month, or even a year. It's not an ingrained talent or gift but the product of hard work and of practicing the habits of inquiry and reflection. As you embark on more advanced scholarly work in the years ahead, you will be assessed on the overall pattern of your work, not on the performance on a single test on a single day in high school. So, relax. At this point, you've done all you can.

Thanks for taking this journey with us, and best of luck!

Answer Keys and Commentaries

KEYS TO PRACTICE EXAM 1

Practice Exam 1 MCQs

Keys and Commentaries

SECTION I

PART A: MULTIPLE CHOICE

1. **A** Initial European exploration focused on trade in various parts of the world. With a few exceptions, the desire to create colonies in Africa occurred during the nineteenth century.

2. **D** Beliefs in European cultural and political superiority led explorers to regard native Africans as a monolithic group and to make enslavement of them an aspect of their trade interests.

3. **B** The protective tariffs under the American system were designed to protect fledgling American industry from foreign competition by making foreign goods more expensive.

4. **A** South Carolina nullified the tariff of 1832, setting in motion the nullification crisis, which eventually led to the Compromise Tariff of 1833.

5. **C** Calhoun believed that protective tariffs benefited Northern industry by placing an excessive tax burden [but not excessive regulations] on Southern agricultural states.

6. **B** Advocates for American Indians, such as Helen Hunt Jackson, saw the Dawes Act as the best hope for American Indians to adjust and assimilate into white society.

7. **C** The allotment of land to heads of households under the Dawes Act left many acres of reservation land undistributed, which were ultimately opened to white settlement. While the Dawes Act's intent was to break down tribal loyalty, it was not successful in accomplishing that aim.

8. **C** Helen Hunt Jackson's *A Century of Dishonor* chronicles the federal government's violations of treaties signed with American Indian tribes.

9. **B** Goldwater and other conservatives believed that the national government's power was limited to only what was specifically given it by the Constitution.

10. **D** Goldwater and other conservatives believed that one of the biggest expenditures of the national government should be for national defense.

11. **A** Goldwater believed that government regulations of the economy or of society would limit citizens' ability to enjoy their freedoms and to pursue their economic goals.

12. **C** Conflict arose between the backcountry residents and the eastern establishment that controlled the government largely because the backcountry felt that their interests were not being adequately addressed by colonial governments.

13. **B** A portion of Bacon's army was made up of freed indentured servants, sometimes called "landless rabble," which led many to fear they could not rely on the indentured servant system to supply adequate labor. This coupled with an increasingly prosperous British economy led to reliance on slave labor.

14. **B** A primary concern for backcountry inhabitants was their view that eastern dominated legislatures were not providing them with adequate protection from American Indians.

15. **D** Calhoun's speech was a turning point in that he presented slavery as a positive good rather than a necessary evil.

16. **A** Southerners increasingly feared slave rebellions, particularly after the Nat Turner revolt in 1831. They also resented the growing activities of abolitionists both inside and outside of Congress.

17. **B** Calhoun meant that because slavery was common in the South but not elsewhere, others did not understand all the factors involved.

18. **C** As Southerners became more dependent on slave labor to keep the cotton economy going, they grew more defensive about efforts to limit both the institution of slavery and its expansion.

19. **B** Thomas Paine was a critic of monarchy and royal power, believing instead that men should rule themselves.

20. **A** Thomas Paine believed a republic allowed men to choose representatives who could make and enforce laws approved by the people. When those representatives failed to uphold the best interests of the people who chose them, they could be turned out of office in a new election, unlike a monarch, who could not be removed.

21. **C** Paine felt the House of Commons was a step in the right direction of a true republic, but he believed the monarchy had too much power over the decisions made by the representatives of the people. He also disapproved of a hereditary monarchy.

22. **A** Enlightenment thinkers advocated for the right of men to form their own governments as well as change them when those governments no longer protected their natural rights as citizens.

23. **B** Vertical integration as well as horizontal integration allowed businesses to consolidate and gain significant share of the market in their respective fields.

24. **D** Unscrupulous and later illegal activities by business leaders were used to gain a competitive advantage by eliminating competition.

25. **B** While Carnegie believed that the wealthy had a duty to use their wealth for the common good, he also believed that the wealthy had been chosen to amass great fortunes because they knew how to use that wealth to benefit the poor better than the poor themselves.

26. **C** The post–World War II baby boom led to teacher shortages and overcrowding in public schools during the 1950s.

27. **D** In many ways the 1950s represented a child-centered society, elevating children's importance as a particularly special generation consisting of the best and brightest.

28. **A** Despite fears of a "population bomb" when baby boomers reached childbearing years, baby boomers had children later in life and fewer in number than the previous generation, leading to what came to be known as the "baby bust" generation.

29. **B** Because many immigrants arrived with little or nothing, many were willing to work for whatever wages they were offered. Employers sometimes turned to these less expensive workers, causing workers who were already employed at higher wages to lose their jobs.

30. **A** Since the 1600s, the United States has always been a nation of immigrants. Those who later were critical of newly arrived immigrants were themselves the descendants of immigrants who came earlier.

31. **B** Native Americans, who were here before British colonization began, were devastated by European immigrants, losing their lands, their traditional cultures, and often their lives. They had to wait centuries before being recognized as citizens in a country built on land that was originally theirs.

32. **D** In an attempt to bolster church membership and declining influence, Puritans adopted the Halfway Covenant, which relaxed requirements for church membership.

33. **D** The agreement to ease requirements for church membership in 1662 became known as the Halfway Covenant.

34. **C** Intolerance of dissenting religious views led people like, but not limited to, Anne Hutchinson and Roger Williams to establish the colony of Rhode Island, where freedom of conscience and separation of church and state became the order of the day.

35. **C** Locke declared that, increasingly, African Americans were refusing to go along with white expectations and demands and were beginning to take control of their own futures.

36. **A** Locke spoke of the "migrant masses shifting from country to city," the Great Migration of the early twentieth century, as spurring a new outlook among the thousands who made this journey.

37. **B** Harlem attracted many who moved North during the Great Migration, and New York City became the heart of a revival of African American arts, literature, economic development, and social institutions during the 1920s, hence the name "Harlem Renaissance."

38. **C** Crevecoeur was impressed with the lack of distinction found among Americans when it came to issues of equality in terms of citizenship and the law. Even though there were differences in wealth, citizens considered themselves equals when it came to their rights as citizens.

39. **B** Crevecoeur believed that society in America had been able to evolve without the assumed barriers of rank and privilege that were so much a part of life in European countries. There was no hereditary status to hold people to one class.

40. **D** Crevecoeur's observations applied to white males. Women, the enslaved, Native Americans, and those without any property were generally treated as less than first-class citizens.

41. **A** NSC-68 reexamined U.S. foreign policy in light of the fact that the Soviet Union had successfully exploded an atomic bomb and that China had fallen to communist forces.

42. **C** NSC-68 concluded that the United States should dramatically accelerate the buildup of nuclear weapons as a deterrent to Soviet expansion. This led to an arms race between the United States and the Soviet Union and fears of mutually assured destruction in the event of an atomic war.

43. **C** Eisenhower warned of the influence and power of the military-industrial complex in determining U.S. foreign policy.

44. **C** The Missouri Compromise declared that all territory north of 36° 30' would be off limits to the expansion of slavery. The Kansas-Nebraska Act opened up the possibility of the spread of slavery through popular sovereignty.

45. **B** Abolitionists vehemently opposed the adoption of popular sovereignty because they wanted no expansion of slavery whatsoever.

46. **A** Fighting broke out almost immediately in Kansas, as both sides of the slavery issue struggled to rush settlers to the area in order to get the upper hand in coming elections.

47. **B** Turner felt the existence of the frontier offered a democratic atmosphere and chance for a new start to all who chose to settle there. He felt that losing this experience would have an impact on the country as it developed into an urban society.

48. **A** The United States launched into an era of overseas expansion, and the country sought to increase its wealth and become a global power. Ideas of moral and cultural superiority characterizing "Manifest Destiny" would be used to justify that expansion.

49. **D** Turner's praise of the democratic atmosphere of the frontier overlooked the almost total disregard for the impact of U.S. expansion on American Indian culture as well as the environmental damage done as the railroads pushed across the prairie.

50. **D** Jackson asserted that the president had an equal right with the courts to determine the constitutionality of federal laws.

51. **C** Jackson's comment concerning the outcome of *Worchester v. Georgia*—"John Marshall has made his decision, now let him enforce it"— indicated an increase in executive power by the decision not to enforce a Supreme Court ruling .

52. **A** The Jacksonian era witnessed movement toward universal white male suffrage through the elimination of property requirements for voting, which democratized the political process.

53. **D** Little Boxes criticized what it believed was the mindless conformity and over-emphasis on materialism during the 1950s.

54. **A** The cookie-cutter houses of Levittowns and suburbs came to symbolize the conformity of American society during the 1950s.

55. **D** Little Boxes most clearly mirrored the Lost Generation's criticism of American society during the 1920s as shallow and superficial.

Practice Exam 1 SAQs

NOTE: Answers to SAQs may vary greatly depending on what students were taught about the topics. The answers provided are suggestions only. Other answers may be deemed correct if they are historically and contextually accurate.

SAQ 1. Possible Answers:

a) Although Hofstadter thought that the Populists wanted to restore the world of the Jeffersonian yeoman farmer, Pollock believed they were trying to adopt reforms that would correct the undemocratic changes that had been caused by industrialization.

b) The development of the railroad placed farmers at the mercy of market forces that made it difficult for them to get out of debt.

c) The Populist Party platform sought democratic reforms, such as public ownership of railroads and telegraph lines, postal savings banks, and graduated income taxes.

SAQ 2. Possible Answers:

a) In the last part of the nineteenth century, the European countries were pursuing imperialist policies and acquiring colonies in Africa and the Pacific.

b) The United States was threatened by powerful European nations for the control of islands in the Caribbean and the Pacific. The U.S. was concerned that it would be limited in trading in those areas.

c) The United States responded by becoming an imperial power and acquiring territories, such as Hawaii and Samoa, and by going to war with Spain and acquiring Puerto Rico, Guam, and the Philippines.

SAQ 3. Possible Answers:

a) The Mississippi River Valley offered opportunities for Native tribes to hunt, fish, and grow crops. They traveled and traded up and down the river and lived in villages in the river valley.

b) The semi-arid climate and the grasslands of the Great Plains made it necessary for Native tribes to follow the buffalo, their food source, and to live in teepees that could be moved from place to place.

c) Tribes in the Eastern woodlands lived in villages in permanent dwellings made of wood, and their access to rivers and the ocean enabled them to farm and fish.

SAQ 4. Possible Answers:

a) The OPEC oil embargo in 1973 and increased pollution because of the lack of regulation of transportation and manufacturing were among the causes for changes in the natural environment.

b) The government's mandate to reduce the speed limit to 55 mph, the increase in the popularity of fuel-efficient smaller cars, especially from Germany and Japan, and the creation of the Environmental Protection Agency were among the actions taken to deal with environmental changes.

c) The United States changed its policies toward the Middle East because the U.S. consumed more oil than it produced and had to negotiate with Arab countries for continued access to oil.

Notes and Commentary on Practice Exam 1 DBQ

Document 1:

Main idea relevant to the question: Bernard Bailyn argues that fear of power is central to shaping American governmental structures after the American Revolution. Even after the ratification of the Constitution, the fear of power shaped the concerns of the Founding Fathers.

Potential example of a statement of the main idea tied directly to the question: Just as the colonists feared the tyrannical power of the government of Great Britain, so too did the postwar years bring controversy between those who feared anarchy and those who feared tyranny.

Potential example of sourcing: Historical situation: The Constitutional Convention came on the heels of an ineffective government in the form of the Articles of Confederation, which lacked the power to tax, regulate interstate commerce, or enforce its laws.

Evidence beyond the documents (outside information): Articles of Confederation, Constitution, Democratic-Republican Societies, Federalists (Party), Antifederalists, Confederal System, Federal System, Separation of Powers.

Document 1: This secondary source, an excerpt by historian Bernard Bailyn, is intended to provide an organizing concept to read and analyze the documents. You should examine each document for the way it addresses concerns about how political power is exercised first in the Articles of Confederation and then during the debates over the Constitution and its ratification by the states. Bailyn argues that newly independent Americans continued to have concerns over placing too much power in the hands of a central government.

Document 2:

Major idea relevant to the question: Henry Knox is complaining of disorder in Massachusetts and of a lack of sufficient power to suppress it.

Potential example of a statement of the main idea tied directly to the question: Following the conclusion of the Revolutionary War, the inability of the Articles of Confederation to generate an adequate source of revenue left the central government largely helpless to respond to civil unrest

Potential example of sourcing: Point of view, historical situation: Knox is complaining that the federal government lacked the resources to maintain order in the United States. His response to Shays's Rebellion reflects and reinforces the concern over the weakness of the Articles of Confederation, which led to the calling of a constitutional convention.

Outside information: Shays's Rebellion, no power to tax, "not worth a Continental."

Document 2: Document 2 is intended to stimulate discussion of the ways in which observers felt that the economic and social problems of the post-revolutionary period were caused by a lack of power in the central government, the Confederation Congress. Pointing to the difficulty of suppressing Shays's Rebellion, Henry Knox is complaining to Washington about the need for a stronger central government.

Document 3:

Major idea relevant to the question: Richard Henry Lee argued against the Constitution because it consolidated too much power in structures of the central government.

Potential example of a statement of the main idea tied directly to the question: Having declared independence from Great Britain because the perceived abuse of power by the central government, many Americans were afraid to give the same powers to new government of the United States, fearing the potential for tyranny.

Potential example of sourcing: Purpose: Lee's opposition to the concentration of power in the central government was part of a widespread propaganda campaign by Antifederalists to secure defeat of the ratification of the Constitution.

Outside information: Antifederalists, Richard Henry Lee (author of the Resolution for Independence), Thomas Jefferson, Edmund Randolph, Bill of Rights.

Document 3: This document represents the intellectual opposition to the Constitution. Richard Henry Lee illustrated the way in which the Antifederalists feared that the new government would essentially replace the tyranny of British imperial government. Lee and the Antifederalists believed that the liberties of Americans could best be defended by their state and local governments.

Document 4:

Major idea relevant to the question: *Federalist 21* justifies the strengthening of the central government by arguing for the necessity of an expansive reading of its powers to compel state governments to support it.

Potential example of a statement of the main idea tied directly to the question: Federalists supported ratification of a constitution that gave the newly created government of the United States the power to enforce its laws, a power that had been lacking under the Articles of Confederation.

Potential example of sourcing: Audience or purpose: The *Federalist Papers* were designed to alleviate the fears of those who questioned increasing the power of the central government and, in particular, to convince New York delegates to the state ratifying convention of the necessity of creating a stronger central government.

Outside information: Imposts, state requisitions, Necessary and Proper or Elastic Clause, Implied Powers, Alexander Hamilton, *Federalist 10*, checks and balances, executive branch.

Document 4: *Federalist 21* illustrates the alignment of both supporters and opponents (Antifederalists) over the ratification of the Constitution. The pamphlet is significant for raising the idea that the new government needed powers, such as the power to tax, to carry out its business. In so doing, it also argues for the need of the enabling or "Necessary and Proper" clause, which supports the doctrine of implied powers that allows the government to carry out policies or powers not specified in the Constitution.

Document 5:

Major idea relevant to the question: "Resolution of the Pennsylvania Minority" points out that a small group of ambitious men had taken control of the convention to ratify the Constitution, contrary to the wishes of the Pennsylvania Assembly.

Potential example of a statement of the main idea tied directly to the question: Some questioned the legitimacy of the Constitution because the Constitutional Convention had exceeded its expressed authorization to only amend the Articles of Confederation, instead of creating an entirely new government.

Potential example of sourcing: Audience or purpose: Opponents of ratification of the Constitution attempted to gain support for its rejection by convincing delegates that the Constitutional Convention had acted inappropriately by exceeding its power and creating a document that could lead to tyranny by possibly by eliminating the government of Pennsylvania.

Outside information: The Constitutional Convention's sole and expressed purpose was to revise the Articles of Confederation.

Document 5: The "Resolution of the Pennsylvania Minority" expresses another form of argument against the ratification of the Constitution and illustrates the significant opposition to the Constitution. Its most potent argument is that the Pennsylvania delegation was not authorized to write a new constitution but to reform the Articles of Confederation. As such, ratification represented an illegitimate exercise of power by a self-interested group. The document also suggests the undemocratic nature of the Constitution.

Document 6:

Major idea relevant to the question: James Madison argues that the desire of government for a national bank is an unwarranted extension of federal power.

Potential example of a statement of the main idea tied directly to the question: Following ratification of the Constitution, conflicting views of the legitimacy of loose or strict interpretations of the Constitution would eventually lead to the formation of the First American Party System consisting of Federalists and Democratic-Republicans.

Potential example of sourcing: Point of view: Madison's view of the Constitution was designed to limit the power of the federal government and convince members of the House of Representatives to vote accordingly. In the end, the Bank of the United States was authorized.

Outside information: First Bank of the United States, Hamilton's "Report on a National Bank," First American Party System, loose vs. strict constructionism, "Necessary and Proper" clause, Alexander Hamilton.

Document 6: Following ratification of the Constitution, political differences led to conflicting interpretations of it. A key figure in this was James Madison, who became concerned about Hamilton's use of the Elastic Clause, which, under a doctrine of loose interpretation, claimed that the implied powers of the Constitution enabled the financial and manufacturing programs Hamilton sought to put in place. Madison argued for limits on the grounds that the Constitution should be read strictly or narrowly. These rival interpretations of the Constitution led to the formation of the First American Party System consisting of Federalists and Democratic-Republicans.

Document 7:

Major idea relevant to the question: Jefferson to Madison praises the rise of the Democratic-Republican Societies to assert the value of democracy and to counteract the political power of the Federalists.

Potential example of a statement of the main idea tied directly to the question: Critics of the power of the federal government saw in it the ability to stifle free speech and elevate the wealthy elite to a position of power that was unattainable by the common man. While Jefferson was most fearful of tyranny, Alexander Hamilton was most fearful of anarchy.

Potential example of sourcing: Point of view: Jefferson was afraid of tyranny if too much power was placed in the hands of the federal government. More a believer in democracy than republicanism, Jefferson sought to convince political leaders of the need to extend the vote to educated common men.

Outside information: Revolution of 1800 (the election of Jefferson), Alien and Sedition Acts, Virginia and Kentucky Resolutions, republicanism, democracy.

Document 7: Jefferson's letter to Madison is intended to elicit a discussion regarding the rise of political parties. The Constitution of 1787 did not envision the existence of political factions. Madison in *Federalist 10* expresses his fear of them, hence the need for checks and balances within government. This letter indicates the way Jefferson has come to rely on political factions—the Democratic-Republican Societies— and campaigning as a means outside the formal structure of the Constitution to check the policies and, by inference, the power of the Federalists whom he and Madison have come to see as passing legislation that favors an upper, monied class (Hamilton's policies on subsidies for manufacturing, the establishment of the Bank of the United States (BUS), and the redemption of the public debt). Political factions need to be organized to check the power of the few in favor of democracy and thus limit the potential for tyranny, too much power, and preserve citizens' rights.

Commentary on Question

Writing a strong essay for this DBQ depends on a clear understanding of the argument that historian Bernard Bailyn presents in Document 1, and any thesis has to consider how it helps to organize the documents and essay. Bailyn argues that the Revolution's obsession with power pervades the immediate post-revolutionary period. The task of the essay then is to demonstrate how the documents support, modify, or qualify this perspective. Each document deals with determining how power is needed to avoid the destabilizing impact of popular, democratic forces or how power has to be limited to prevent the restoration of an oppressive government. One approach to the question is to use the extent to which the documents reflect a concern with the exercise of power and the impact it had over the period 1783 to 1800. Documents 2 and 4 should help you document the need for the Constitution of 1787 with central government possessed of more robust power. Documents 3 and 5 illustrate fears that too much power was being given to the central government and that the new ratifying process might be aimed at suppressing the rights of a broader, more democratic population. In this instance, Shays's Rebellion in Document 2 can also help in suggesting that the conflict is between the few and the many, that the latter has also been victimized by taxes and the foreclosure of family farms that benefited the few. Documents 3 and 5 also speak to the fear that local interests and minority rights might be suppressed when the new constitutional government falls into the hands of a few unprincipled men. Countering Lee (Document 2) and the Pennsylvania minority (Document 4), you also have ample opportunity to provide evidence beyond the documents that would greatly enhance the argument and reasoning of your essay with commentary on either *Federalist 10*, arguing the internal structure of the Constitution provides checks and balances on the potential abuse of power, or the provision of the Bill of Rights as a compromise to assure the Antifederalists of the existence of specific limits on the national government's powers. Documents 6 and 7 illustrate the persistence of the fear of central government power. Madison attempted to deal with the problems of the new nation's economy (Hamilton's economic programs, especially the BUS and the Reports on Manufacturing and Public Credit are good examples of supporting evidence beyond the documents). Madison's reversal leads to his political realignment with Jefferson and the rise of the Democratic-Republican Societies as a democratic counterweight to what they saw as the Federalists' abuse of power for their self-interest. Noting that Madison not only reverses his positions supporting the Constitution but explicitly modifies his fear of political factions in *Federalist 10* also provides the basis for a highly nuanced, complex essay.

Another approach to this DBQ is to focus on Bailyn's suggestion of the conflict over political power "from populist forces and local interests that threatened not only the welfare of local property owners and defenders of the rule of law." In this approach, the instability of the post-revolutionary period provided the context for reforming the Articles of Confederation characterizing the Constitution as a structure designed to protect property rights of the wealthy. It might be useful to think about how the flow of documents can lead you to Document 7 with its substantiation of the belief in the need for democratic action through political parties to offset the Constitution's favoring of local property holders. Using this thread, the protection of slave property and the power to tax so as to be able to redeem the national debt can be useful pieces of outside information that substantiate the Constitution as a document protecting property rights in opposition to the more populist, democratic interests represented by Shays's Rebellion in Document 2. The poor Shaysites illustrate people burdened with debt and taxes who protest state policies favoring the wealthy. Their protests frighten people like Knox, who assert that the protests caused social and economic instability that had led to violence and threatened the survival of an independent United States, which then justified the calling of the Constitution Convention. Documents 3 and 5, Richard Henry Lee challenges the need for a central government, substantiates the existence of local interests that were, in his opinion, more democratic and that did not feel the need for change. Although Document 5 might be partially misleading—it is a minority report—its argument that the majority was, in fact, wrong, that its decision was not authorized by the Pennsylvania Assembly and therefore was not representative of Pennsylvanians. Documents 4, 6, and 7 raise the tension between democracy and the few property owners because of the federal government's use of implied consent, of the "Necessary and Proper" clause, to pass legislation that seemed to favor a few property owners. The most obvious example of this was Hamilton's fiscal program, the Reports on the National Bank, Manufacturing, and Public Debt, to which Madison and

APPENDIX : ANSWER KEYS AND COMMENTARIES

Jefferson objected. The objections took two forms. In Document 6 Madison argues against the program on the grounds that the "Necessary and Proper" clause (Document 4) was inappropriately used, that it abused the powers the Constitution, and led him to advocate for a theory of strict construction or interpretation that would limit the Constitution's powers. Jefferson in Document 7 should key a discussion of the sifting out of interests and factions into what became the first party system, the division between the more hierarchical and elitist Federalists and the Democratic-Republicans which theoretically represented the ways in which interests divided in the national government and led to the election of Jefferson in 1800.

Possible examples to earn the complexity of understanding point for the overall essay:

- In order to earn the complexity point, your essay might examine how ideas about the distribution of political power continued to define the structure and function of the federal government during the Nullification Crisis and/or the Civil War.

- In order to earn the complexity point, your essay might examine how regional economic and social interests, rather than political philosophy, colored varying views of the distribution of power between the federal and state governments.

APPENDIX : ANSWER KEYS AND COMMENTARIES

Notes and Commentaries for Practice Exam 1 LEQs

Question 2. Evaluate the extent to which religion (religious fervor) fostered change in American society between 1730 and 1770.

Thesis and Contextualization

The increasingly diverse makeup of the British North American colonies seemed to lead to declining religious fervor among eighteenth-century colonists. Accommodations such as the Halfway Covenant in New England, which had eased rigid requirements for church membership, suggested a weakening of religious belief. In addition, the expanding population of the colonies meant that the backcountry did not get access to ministers and priests. What emerged was a more emotional-based religion that challenged established religious authority, expanded higher education, and divided denominations.

Evidence and Analysis and Reasoning

The following examples may be included but are not limited to:

- The Great Awakening resulted in a more evangelical (emotional) delivery of religious teachings.

- Itinerant preachers like Jonathan Edwards and George Whitefield held religious revivals and camp meetings that brought religion to the backcountry as well as to established communities.

- Conflict between the established, rationally based religious leaders and more evangelical preachers led to the division of many denominations into "New Light" (New Side) and "Old Light" (Old Side) factions and frequently led to separate congregations in settled areas.

- The increasing number of denominations required the establishment of institutions of higher learning, such as Dartmouth, Brown, and Princeton, or Log Cabin Colleges, to train ministers.

- Challenges to traditional authority led to an increased sense of individualism.

Complexity point

- Discuss how, challenging religious authority led to challenging political authority and to the American Revolution.

- Discuss how, despite changes brought on by the Great Awakening, long-established churches continued to maintain significant levels of membership and continued to have considerable influence in both the political and the social arena.

Question 3. Evaluate the extent to which religion (religious fervor) fostered change in American society between 1800 and 1850.

Thesis and Contextualization

Following the War of 1812, emotional American nationalism peaked during the Era of Good Feeling. Similarly, the "rise of the common man" during the Age of Jackson led to increasingly emotionalized campaigning as a means of attracting average citizens to the political arena. Not surprisingly, religious emotionalism reached a fever pitch during this period as well. Although some historians place the start of this phenomenon with the Cane Ridge Revival in 1801, its most significant impact on American society occurred from 1820 to 1850 with the establishment of reform movements, the development of perfectionist communities, and the movement's growing impact on the debate over slavery.

Evidence and Analysis and Reasoning

The following examples may be included but are not limited to:

- The Second Great Awakening sparked an evangelical emotional religious revival spurred on by people like Charles Grandison Finney and Theodore Frelinghuysen, who emphasized "heart" rather than "mind" (philosophical) religion.

- The Erie Canal and the "burned over region" of New York became a conduit for the spread of reform in American society.

- The Second Great Awakening's belief in the perfectibility of man spawned movements for prison reform (the Auburn and Pennsylvania systems), better treatment of the insane (Dorothea Dix), temperance (Washington Temperance Society, "teetotalism"), and the abolition of slavery (William Lloyd Garrison, Frederick Douglass).

- The Second Great Awakening also spurred the development of "utopian communitarianism" and the formation of religious enclaves (Shakers, Millerites, Mormons), economic experimentation (New Harmony, Owenites), perfectionist communities (Oneida), and intellectual communities (Brook Farm).

- The increased sense of individualism also led to demands for the elimination of societal constraints on individuals (Seneca Falls Convention, Elizabeth Cady Stanton) and the growth of public education (Horace Mann).

Complexity point

- Discuss how the impact of the first industrial revolution led to population concentrations, made social problems more visible, and seemed to cause a breakdown in morality.

- Discuss how the Second Great Awakening was connected to the rise of Romanticism and Transcendentalism.

Question 4. Evaluate the extent to which religion (religious fervor) fostered change in American society between 1970 and 1990.

The 1960s represented a dramatic liberalization of American society and culture. The rise of a youth counterculture and social reforms that seemed to undermine the Protestant work ethic, and challenges to traditional family values and structures, led many Americans to question the direction of liberal reform. Against this backdrop, evangelical and traditional fundamentalists looked to stem the tide by becoming politically active as a voting bloc. The power of a political bloc of highly organized and motivated Christian fundamentalists altered the political spectrum of American politics, led to organized attempts to legislate morality, and elevated religious leaders to political power brokers who could to some degree dictate policy.

APPENDIX : ANSWER KEYS AND COMMENTARIES

Evidence and Analysis and Reasoning

The following examples may be included but are not limited to:

- The rise of the counterculture during the 1960s led conservative fundamentalists to question the direction of society and challenge some of the social norms that had emerged (Stonewall riots, gay rights).

- The religious right began to question the expanded role of women beyond that of wives and homemakers (ERA, STOP ERA, NOW, Phyllis Schlafly); failure of ERA; threats to abortion rights.

- Evangelical religious leaders encouraged their congregations to demand that politicians incorporate moral values into legislation (Jerry Falwell, Pat Robertson, Moral Majority, Christian Coalition, antiabortion, school prayer, *Roe v. Wade*).

- Fundamentalists founded new universities to instill the values of scriptural literalism (Liberty University, Oral Roberts University, Bob Jones University).

- The fundamentalist right increasingly used television evangelism to mobilize and motivate its political base (*700 Club*, mega-churches).

Complexity point

- Examine the impact of the Christian right on politics.

- Examine the irony of the acceptance of greater diversity with the political influence of the "moral majority."

KEYS TO PRACTICE EXAM 2

Practice Exam 2 MCQs

Keys and Commentaries

SECTION I

PART A MULTIPLE CHOICE

1. **B** Columbus saw both beauty and potential for farming, cattle raising, and development in the lands he found. Economic and political control over the lands would eventually come.

2. **C** Columbus held some respect for the Native peoples he encountered even though he believed they were inferior. He failed to see the diversity among the cultures of the Native people.

3. **A** Slave purchasers did not want to buy slaves who might have been exposed to diseases like smallpox because that threatened their investment.

4. **C** Many slaves were first brought from Africa to the West Indies, where plantation owners worked to break their spirits and train them to do the expected work. That made the slaves more valuable for later sale in North America.

5. **B** This man has managed to learn some of two different languages while enslaved. He has also made his escape, taking a weapon and ammunition along with him.

6. **B** The Antiquities Act was an example of government protection of national treasures. There had been particular concern about the looting of Indian artifacts for profit.

7. **A** The President could name structures or sites as national monuments at his discretion. The government could acquire sites on private land.

8. **C** Preservation programs were meant to provide complete protection to an area or site. Conservation programs allowed controlled management and use of a natural resource.

9. **C** The massive increase in Irish and German immigration during the 1840s and 1850s saw the rise of Nativist sentiment similar to what Morse was expressing in the passage.

10. **C** Increased Nativist sentiment led to the rise of the American or Know Nothing Party, which nominated Millard Fillmore for president in 1856.

11. **D** The late nineteenth century saw a dramatic increase in the volume of immigrants entering the United States and a fundamental shift in the areas of Europe from which they came.

12. **C** With the collapse and disbanding of the Soviet Union, the Cold War that had begun after World War II was at an end. Nuclear weapons and Russian communism still existed in the world, but the Soviet Union has dissolved.

13. **D** President Bush saw the importance of the United States working with other nations and leading the drive for world peace.

14. **A** In the 1990s, the "enemies" of the United States—many "terrorist" groups—threatened the U.S. and the world, but often they were difficult to identify and to track.

15. **A** King Philip asserted that there was initially a degree of compatibility between English settlers and Native tribes.

16. **B** The Pequot War and King Philip's War are the two major, but not the only, examples of military conflict between the colonists and American Indians prior to the French and Indian War. Similar conflicts occurred outside of New England in other British North American colonies.

17. **A** The leading cause of conflict between the colonists and American Indians throughout the British North American colonies was the colonists' encroachment on Indian lands.

18. **B** The Compromise of 1850 included the Fugitive Slave Law, which gave federal support to slave owners hoping to recapture runaway slaves who had managed to get to Northern states.

19. **B** Massachusetts was where many of the earliest events of the American Revolution took place, and many people, such as the men named, felt that real independence meant an end to slavery.

20. **A** This call to action is an example of nullification, a situation in which a state declares it will not abide by a federal law it feels is illegal or unjust.

21. **B** Nixon's speech was aimed at winning the votes of the "silent majority" of American blue-collar workers who were disenchanted with social unrest in the country.

22. **C** The movement of the mainstream Democratic Party toward a more liberal social welfare program alienated conservative Southern Democrats and led to the breakup of the "solid" South, traditionally the stronghold of the Democratic Party.

23. **B** Nationally televised protests and the resulting violence at the Democratic National Convention over a number of issues led the Democratic Party to appear to be in disarray.

24. **D** The Knights of Labor created one big union comprised of both skilled and unskilled workers, and they sought the establishment of a "just and harmonious society."

25. **B** Despite their efforts, the Knights of Labor were largely unsuccessful in significantly improving the lives of workers. The demise of the Knights of Labor came in part as a result of the Haymarket Square incident, and the group had died out by the turn of the twentieth century.

26. **A** The American Federation of Labor focused more than the Knights of Labor on concrete goals of higher wages, shorter hours, and better working conditions, which became known as bread and butter unionism.

27. **B** Because the North American colonies were expected to support British imperial plans, they were constantly involved in wars with different European countries in the eighteenth century.

28. **D** Franklin was basically proposing what became known as Home Rule, independence in many aspects of government but retaining an alliance with Great Britain.

29. **A** Franklin was a proponent of Enlightenment ideals, and he believed the best government was one that was chosen by the people to represent their interests.

30. **C** Lincoln felt the war was being waged not only to restore the union but also to guarantee that the country would be a place of equality and freedom for all who lived there. He saw their efforts as still being "unfinished business."

31. **C** The phrase ". . . all men are created equal" comes from the Declaration of Independence.

32. **B** At the time of the Gettysburg Address, Lincoln had issued the Preliminary Emancipation Proclamation. The final proclamation would be announced on January 1, 1863. Lincoln stressed "a new birth of freedom" as well as equality for all men in his address.

33. **A** All of these difficulties were common experiences of African Americans living in the Deep South.

34. **C** The U.S. Armed Forces were segregated, so few African Americans were drafted early in the war. The job openings left by white workers who did go to war presented opportunities for those who migrated North.

35. **B** Many African Americans found that racism was not exclusively a Southern trait. Though the Jim Crow system was less in evidence in other parts of the country, discrimination still existed on many levels.

36. **A** Although Eli Whitney is most noted for the invention of the cotton gin, his development of the concept of interchangeable parts stimulated the development of industry in the United States.

37. **B** In the Lowell System utilized in New England textile factories, local farm girls were a source of labor before immigrant sources of labor became readily available.

38. **C** Revolution in transportation allowed faster access to natural resources and markets while agricultural innovation freed up workers who previously had to provide food for themselves.

39. **C** Carnegie's message carries with it the inference that the wealthy achieve success because they are the "fittest" of the human species.

40. **C** Carnegie believed that the wealthy had a duty to use their wealth for philanthropic ventures rather than ostentatious displays of wealth known as conspicuous consumption.

41. **A** Carnegie believed that the wealthy had a better sense of how to use their wealth most effectively to help the poor. Rather than providing direct relief for the poor, he believed that true philanthropy should be designed to assist the poor in advancing themselves through the acquisition of skills and knowledge.

42. **C** The political cartoon features a caricature of Joseph McCarthy, who claimed to have the names of communist infiltrators in the U.S. government during the post–World War II red scare.

43. **C** Ultimately McCarthy was discredited and censured by the Senate as a result of the Army McCarthy hearings.

44. **A** Throughout U.S. history, particularly in times of war, national emergencies generally result in a constriction of civil liberties, particularly the rights to freedom of speech and freedom of the press.

45. **B** Many of the country's anti-imperialists promoted the idea that the United States would be flooded with immigrants seeking jobs or sanctuary to escape poverty in their own lands.

46. **B** Many workers feared that immigrants might be willing to work for lower wages and undercut the job market. Others were concerned about losing the white, Anglo-Saxon Protestant majority in the country to immigrants of different races and religions.

47. **D** Congress passed the 1921 Immigration Quota Act and the 1924 National Origins Act, both of which sharply reduced the numbers of people who were allowed to immigrate to the United States.

48. **B** Frederick Douglass gave his full support to the Seneca Falls Movement, attending the meetings himself.

49. **D** Douglass regretted that some abolitionists he knew had given up working for the end of slavery because they worried that they would also be expected to support full political rights for women.

50. **A** Douglass spoke in support for the Enlightenment concept that people had the right to have a say in how they are governed.

51. **B** The oversized "infant" portrays American industry as having outgrown its need for government protection in the form of protective tariffs.

52. **D** During the Gilded Age, disadvantaged groups, such as the Populist and Granger movements, looked to the federal government for protection from the perceived abuses of big business. Such agitation resulted in the first forms of business regulation: the Interstate Commerce Act and the Sherman Anti-Trust Act.

53. **A** The federal government took the first halting steps to regulate big business in the form of the Interstate Commerce Act and the Sherman Anti-Trust Act. Although both measures tended to be weakly enforced, they nevertheless signaled increased willingness on the part of the federal government to regulate business.

54. **D** Reagan's economic policy included lowering taxes for the highest-income Americans and eliminating many government regulations on American businesses.

55. **A** The conservative political movement of the 1980s and beyond favored a much more limited role for the national government.

APPENDIX : ANSWER KEYS AND COMMENTARIES

Practice Exam 2 SAQs

NOTE: Answers to SAQs may vary greatly depending on what students were taught about the topics. The answers provided are suggestions only. Other answers may be deemed correct if they are historically and contextually accurate.

SAQ 1. Possible Answers:

a) Bowers' excerpt calls the Radical Republican leaders of Reconstruction selfish, corrupt, and brutal men whose policies abused Southerners and whose actions misled Northerners into thinking the Radicals were patriotic leaders. Foner's excerpt says that the Radical leaders' intentions were to change the nation by using a strong national government to protect civil rights of all citizens.

b) The 14th and 15th Amendments granting citizenship and voting rights to Freedmen support Foner's view that the Radicals were devoted to ensuring civil rights for all.

c) Both excerpts see Reconstruction as revolutionary because it led to an increase in power of the national government and made changes in the South after slavery was abolished.

SAQ 2. Possible Answers:

a) O'Sullivan meant that the United States had a God-given right to expand its control over the North American continent and to spread its democracy into newly acquired territories.

b) The excerpt showed concern that foreign nations were threatening to interfere in Texas and to prevent the United States from fulfilling its destiny to control the continent.

OR

The natural resources and the available land in the western part of the continent presented opportunities for American settlers and enhanced the economy of the country.

c) The United States acquired new territories, such as Texas, California, and the Southwest in the 1840s, then had to determine whether slavery would be allowed into the newly acquired territories.

SAQ 3. Possible Answers:

a) As the British colonies fought for their independence, their "freedoms," and their "rights," many questioned how slavery in the colonies could be justified. The Enlightenment ideals that influenced the declaring of independence recognized the value of the individual. Many in America believed that slavery robbed people of their value and rights.

b) After they declared independence, the states began writing their own constitutions. In Northern states, those constitutions called for the elimination of slavery or made slavery illegal. Even Southern states put restrictions on the continuation of the slave trade. When the U.S. Constitution was written in 1787, it contained a provision that Congress could make no law concerning the slave trade until 1808.

c) The invention of the cotton gin in the 1790s and the growing national and international demand for cotton caused Southern states to rely more on slavery, and thus the number of slaves increased.

SAQ 4. Possible Answers:

a) Both the New Deal and the Great Society were domestic programs that empowered the national government of the United States to create a safety net to aid people in overcoming economic hardships.

OR

Both the New Deal and the Great Society enlarged the scope of the national government by creating agencies dealing with social and economic conditions of the American people.

b) Social Security, which provides unemployment and retirement benefits for Americans, is a program created as part of the New Deal.

OR

The New Deal included federally funded jobs programs, such as the Works Progress Administration, to provide work for people during the Great Depression.

c) Medicare, which provides health insurance and medical care for senior Americans, is a program created as part of the Great Society.

OR

The Great Society created federal programs such as Head Start to help eliminate poverty in the United States.

Notes and Commentary for Practice Exam 2 DBQ

Document 1:

Major idea relevant to the question: "Old Rhyme—New Reason" sums up the defeat of the Treaty of Versailles because of the Republicans' addition of amendments restricting U.S. involvement in the League of Nations and Wilson's refusal to allow consideration of them in the final vote.

Potential example of a statement of the main idea directly tied to the question: Disillusionment over the failure of World War I to realize its idealistic goals led the United States to a more isolationistic position in world affairs, as the U.S. Senate rejected the Treaty of Versailles and membership in the League of Nations.

Potential example of sourcing: Historical situation: Woodrow Wilson's insistence on embedding the League of Nations Charter in the Treaty of Versailles led reservationists, concerned over Article X, to reject the treaty.

Outside information: Isolationism; to Make the World Safe for Democracy; War to End All War; Irreconcilables; William Borah; Fourteen Points.

Document 1: is the kind of ambiguous document that illustrates the complexity of the historical problem. The document illustrates the demise of the Treaty of Versailles and support for the League of Nations. The image, however, is a bit misleading. Although it makes clear that the Senate was responsible for the rejection of the treaty, part of the reason for that rejection was Wilson's (the crying fly of the illustration) refusal to accept reservations of any kind. Still, the sympathy for the League and future involvement of Americans in world affairs is expressed by the unfavorable portrayal of Senator Lodge strutting in a frock coat. This contrasts especially with Documents 2, 3, 4, and 5, which hold more isolationist positions.

Document 2:

Major idea relevant to the question: *The Nation* illustrates writers' and intellectuals' deep regret with American involvement in World War I, suggesting that nothing was accomplished by the conflict and that the world was again likely to descend into war.

Potential example of a statement of the main idea directly tied to the question: Writers and intellectuals, disillusioned by the fact that World War I was a failed ideological crusade, suggested that U.S. involvement in European affairs was futile and counterproductive.

Potential example of sourcing: Point of view: Intellectual arguments against U.S. involvement in foreign affairs helped swing public opinion toward isolationism and supported the foreign policy of Republican administrations during the 1920s.

Outside information: Isolation, Lost Generation (F. Scott Fitzgerald, Ernest Hemingway, Sinclair Lewis); disarmament; Washington Naval Conference, Five Power Treaty, Four Power Treaty; Kellogg-Briand Pact.

Document 2: makes a more explicit case for disillusionment with the Treaty of Versailles and speaks for a more broadly-based argument for staying out of European affairs. It especially condemns the way in which the treaty demonstrates the frustration of the idealism that seemed to have marked America's entry into the war because it seems as that the conditions for war remained.

Document 3:

Major idea relevant to the question: The image illustrates the use of high tariffs as barriers to express American isolationist feelings. The Fordney-McCumber tariff was designed to protect American industries against Europeans.

Potential example of sourcing: Historical situation: Postwar depression and the Republican desire to "return to [the] normalcy" of the Gilded Age led the United States to erect the highest protective tariff barriers, to that point, in its history.

Outside information: "The business of America is business"; Dawes Plan; Young Plan, Hawley-Smoot Tariff; "return to normalcy."

Document 3: illustrates the impact of tariff policies on American attitudes toward Europe. The Fordney-McCumber tariff was part of generally high tariff policies meant to favor American industries. The tariffs generally inhibited European and especially German economic recovery, making it more difficult for Germany to meet its reparation payments. The sign in the upper right corner and the question "Where does it bend?" confirms Document 2's sense of isolationist sentiments and extends it into the economic sphere. Complicating this idea, however, is the way in which tariff policy and that toward Latin America demonstrated the ways in which the United States intervened when it was economically advantageous to do so.

Document 4:

Major idea relevant to the question: As Europe began to rearm, isolationist elements in Congress arranged for the passage of the Neutrality Act to foreclose the possibility of American intervention in a possible new war.

Potential example of a statement of the main idea directly tied to the question: Determined not to involve itself in another European war as the political situation in Europe deteriorated, Congress enacted neutrality legislation banning the sale of weapons to belligerents.

Potential example of sourcing: Historical situation: The rise of strong dictatorships in Europe, Japanese aggression in the Far East, and the ineffectiveness of the League of Nations led Congress to enact neutrality legislation designed to keep the United States out of involvement in potential hostilities.

Outside information: Kellogg-Briand Pact; Stimson Doctrine; Japanese invasion of Manchuria.

Document 4: is intended to illustrate growing concerns over the remilitarization of Europe and presents an ironic, ambiguous document. Although it seems starkly isolationist—prohibiting the sale of arms to any belligerent nation—it also represents that there were situations where the United States might consider intervening and allowing the sale of arms. Two years later, a Neutrality Act would affirm the prohibition of the sale of arms to Spain but provided the possibility of direct sales at the discretion of the president (Cash and Carry) as a concession to Roosevelt and in response to Japanese expansion into China.

Document 5:

Major idea relevant to the question: The Nye Report charged arms manufacturers in both Europe and the United States with having vested interests in encouraging war because war helps boost sales. The report further argued that arms manufacturers were able to corrupt government officials to sell weapons and thus contribute to the heightening possibility of war.

Potential example of a statement of the main idea directly tied to the question: The Nye committee characterized arms manufacturers as "merchants of death" and reinforce the position of isolationists.

Potential example of sourcing: Point of view: The Nye committee took the position that the United States entered World War I as a result of being duped by the "merchants of death," arms and munitions manufacturers who stood to profit from U.S. involvement in the war. The public report helped push the determination of the American people to remain out of foreign conflicts.

Outside information: "merchants of death"; Quarantine Speech, cash and carry, Lend-Lease, Destroyer Deal, Munich Agreement, appeasement, Spanish Civil War.

Document 5: the Nye Report, investigated the role of munitions manufacturers in World War I. A highly partisan report, it was intended to justify neutrality in future European wars. The report charged that munitions manufacturers especially had a vested interest in selling arms beyond the needs of countries and thereby contributed to an arms race. The incentives also included inducing the countries to buy through the use of corruption, bribery, fear, and hostility. The resulting arms race resulted in economic strain or collapse or precipitated armed conflict. An inference of the arguments of the Nye Report is that it reflected isolationist sentiments like those that produced the Neutrality Acts.

Document 6:

Major idea relevant to the question: In meeting with the Japanese ambassador, Cordell Hull was trying to negotiate an agreement with Japan that would recognize American interests in China.

Potential example of a statement of the main idea directly tied to the question: Fears of aggressive Japanese tendencies in the Far East led many Americans to believe that the time had come for the United States to abandon an isolationist stance and stand firm in defending its interests, as first enunciated in the Open Door Policy.

Potential example of sourcing: Historical situation: As relations between China and Japan deteriorated, the U.S. moved to protect its interests in the Western Pacific.

Outside information: Open Door Notes; Japan's takeover of Manchuria; Japanese invasion of China; Panay Affair; the Philippines.

Document 6: the memorandum, summarizes a meeting of Secretary of State Cordell Hull with the Japanese ambassador to Great Britain and sums up the growing clash of interests between Japan and the United States in the western Pacific. Although the memorandum is couched in friendly terms, both Hull and Yoshida are discussing the clash of interests in Japanese ambitions for expansion into East Asia in search of raw materials and U.S. concern for continued access to China. It also complicates American isolationist policies by demonstrating that the United States has an active, interventionist policy in the Far East: maintaining American commercial interests in China and deterring Japanese expansion.

Document 7:

Major idea relevant to the question: Archibald MacLeish is criticizing American intellectuals who in their disillusionment with World War I contributed to America's isolationist policies. By not supporting a more interventionist policy, MacLeish argues, they allowed the rise of fascism.

Potential example of a statement of the main idea directly tied to the question: With the outbreak of World War II, many Americans followed Roosevelt's lead in believing that the United States had a moral obligation to abandon isolationism and come to the aid of those opposing aggressor nations.

Potential example of sourcing: Purpose: After the outbreak of World War II, MacLeish, like Roosevelt, believed that authors and intellectuals had a duty to abandon isolationism and defend the democracies of Western Europe. His writings were designed to move public opinion away from the position espoused by the America First Committee and toward the open involvement of the United States in the war.

Outside information: America First Committee; Charles Lindbergh; Cash and Carry; Lend-Lease; Destroyer Deal, Arthur Vandenberg, Axis Powers, Allies; fascism.

Document 7: is intended to stimulate a discussion that contrasts with Document 1 and complicates Document 2. MacLeish, a noted literary critic, here connects the changes that occurred between the 1920s and 1930s. The feelings of isolationism and disillusion among writers and scholars, such as the author of Document 2, had evolved by 1940 to arguments for a more active intervention in world affairs to halt the spread of fascism, Nazism, and Japanese imperialism.

Commentary on the Question

This prompt asks you to evaluate the changes in American attitudes toward engagement in world affairs between World Wars I and II. Generally and simplistically, American attitudes during the period 1919 to 1940 are characterized as ones that move from desires for isolation to involvement in global affairs. As this interpretation is generally presented, Americans, disillusioned by the way in which the Treaty of Versailles seemed to allow for the continuation of the same forces that had led to World War I, withdrew from global affairs until the aggression of the Axis Powers and especially Germany and Japan led them to reconsider their positions and begin a more active, interventionist foreign policy. This approach would trace the evolution of isolationism to Archibald MacLeish's call for intellectuals to wake up to the threats of Fascism on the eve of America's entry into World War II. The documents, however, should lead you to a more complicated explanation that could focus either upon 1) the changing nature of ideas towards involvement in world affairs, 2) the continuous, although less noticed, involvement in Europe and Asia especially, or 3) some combination of interpretations 1) and 2). Document 1(Old Rhyme) illustrates the rejection of the treaty by the Republican-dominated senate led by Henry Cabot Lodge and thus a political defeat for President Woodrow Wilson who wanted the U.S. to remain involved in world affairs through the League of Nations. The League of Nations was a centerpiece of Wilson's Fourteen Points and intended to encourage global cooperation and prevent future wars through the arbitration of international disputes. Isolationism is further substantiated by Documents 2 (*The Nation*), 3 (The Fordney-McCumber Tariff), and 5 ("The Nye Report"). Each makes the case for disillusionment with Europe and a desire to stay out of its affairs. Document 2 illustrates writers' and intellectuals' frustration with the futility of the idealism with which Americans had entered the war ("the next war is on the way"); 3 illustrates the desire for economic isolation; 5 blames the World War on the profiteering of munitions manufacturers as a warning against being dragged into international affairs. Document 6 (Conversation with the Japanese Ambassador) is intended to pose a modification on or challenge to the isolationist thesis: that either emerging threats of war in Asia prompted intervention or that there was continued, ongoing American involvement in international affairs. Note that Cordell Hull is trying to negotiate recognition of Americans and Japanese spheres of interest in order to minimize the possibility for conflict. There are multiple ways for analyzing this document by understanding its larger context: that the U.S. already has spheres of influence or that it is responding to events. It substantiates the facts that the U.S. was actively involved in Latin America and the Far East, the latter especially in light of its possession of the Philippines and its interests culturally and economically in China. The document can also stimulate a discussion of continued U.S. involvement in European affairs as demonstrated by things like the Washington Naval Arms Agreement (to limit the size of navies) and the Kellogg-Briand Pact, the signatories of which agreed not to conduct aggressive war. Documents 1 and 4 (The Neutrality Act) also complicate the story. The cartoon in Document 1 is also a critique of isolationism in that Lodge and the Republican reservations, both seen in a critical light (Sourcing and Point of View). Document 4 actually points to growing recognition that events in the world were getting out of hand and that it was necessary to set the terms for American military assistance (See also how it recognizes the isolationist sentiments of the Nye Report and modifies them by allowing for the sale of arms under certain conditions). Document 7 (Archibald MacLeish) illustrates the shift away from isolationism and contrasts directly with Document 2. A strong essay will also place Document 7 in context noting that he is writing when the U.S. is actively supporting Britain's war effort with Lend Lease, patrolling the North Atlantic to support the British navy, and selling it ships, and trying to curb Japanese expansion into China (Document 6).

Possible examples of complexity of understanding point for the overall essay:

- In order to earn the complexity point, your essay might examine how and why post–World War II American attitudes toward the proper role of the United States in world affairs was fundamentally different from post—World War I attitudes.

- In order to earn the complexity point, your essay might examine the role of technology and propaganda in either sustaining or changing American attitudes concerning the proper role of the United States in world affairs.

APPENDIX : ANSWER KEYS AND COMMENTARIES

Notes and Commentaries for Practice Exam 2 LEQS

2. Evaluate the causes that led some of the newly independent states to question the appropriate role of the central government between 1783 and 1800.

Thesis and Contextualization

During the American Revolution, the 13 British colonial governments united to fight the British. Each colony was represented in the Second Continental Congress, which served as a central government for conducting the war, forming an alliance with the French, and making peace. The Continental Congress formed a committee that drafted the Articles of Confederation creating a central government with limited powers that was ratified by the states. Several issues arose between 1783 and 1800 that caused state leaders to question what the role of the central government should be, how much power the central government should have, and how much power the state governments should maintain.

Evidence, Analysis, and Reasoning

The following examples may be included but are not limited to:

- Treaty of Paris of 1783 establishing independence and expanding U.S. territory to the Mississippi River

- Presence of British troops in the Northwest raising the question of what role the central government should play in negotiating or using other means to have them removed

- The central government's role in determining a policy for western land claimed by some states—Land Ordinances of 1784 and 1785 and the Northwest Ordinance

- Payment of debts owed both by the central government and by some of the state governments

- Shays's Rebellion of 1786–1787 causing some to favor strengthening the power of the central government at the expense of the states

- Constitutional Convention of 1787 creating the federalist system and establishing compromises concerning the roles of the central government and the state governments

- Ratification of the Constitution, revealing the objections of some to the increased role of the central government

- Bill of Rights protecting individual and state rights from the central government

- Rise of political parties in the 1790s; Hamiltonian Federalists and Jeffersonian Republicans divided in part over the role and power of the central government and of the states

- Loose versus strict interpretation of the Constitution

- Whiskey Rebellion of 1794 causing some to question the actions of the central government in suppressing the rebellion.

- Alien and Sedition Acts of 1798 causing criticism of the central government's restrictions on state and individual rights leading to the Virginia and Kentucky Resolutions of 1798 arguing states' power to restrict actions of the central government

- "Revolution of 1800," which focused on the issue of the power and role of the central government

Complexity point

- Compare the questioning of the role of the central government between 1783 and 1800 with concerns expressed by the South in the antebellum period over the role of the central government regarding slavery.

- Find similarities in how some states in the late twentieth and early twenty-first century questioned the role of the central government: rise of the conservative movement, abortion rights, gun control versus gun rights, etc.

- Discuss the role of the Supreme Court in various eras in deciding the proper role of the central government.

3. Evaluate the causes that led the South to question the appropriate role of the central government between 1820 and 1860.

Thesis and Contextualization

During the American Revolution and the writing of and debate over the Constitution, some questioned whether slavery could be justified. Americans were fighting the British for freedom and their rights, so how could the institution of slavery, which denied freedom and rights, continue to exist? In the 1790s, the Jeffersonian Republicans spoke for the "sturdy, independent farmer," especially in the South and the West, and they were suspicious of a strong central government that might threaten their independence. With the invention of the cotton gin and the growth of the cotton industry during the Market Revolution, slavery had grown and become an integral part of the economy and society of the South. Issues like the tariff and the rise of abolitionism intensified the debate over states' rights versus federal government power. Southerners became more suspicious of the role of the central government, which they saw as a threat to slavery and southern interests in the 1820 to 1860 period leading to the South's secession from the United States and its government and the Civil War that followed.

Evidence, Analysis, and Reasoning

The following examples may be included but are not limited to:

- Growth of the cotton industry and the increased dependence on slave labor in the South during the Market Revolution

- Passage of tariff laws designed to protect domestic industry and opposed by the agricultural South during the 1820s and 1830s

- John C. Calhoun's *South Carolina Exposition and Protest* of 1828 proposing the theories of nullification of federal laws by the states and secession

- Webster-Hayne debate over states' rights versus federal power in 1830

- South Carolina's nullification of the federal tariff in 1832

- Southern opposition to efforts by slavery opponents to use the power of the central government to prohibit slavery in newly acquired territories in the West

- Southern support for increasing central government power to pass and enforce a fugitive slave law in the Compromise of 1850

- Dred Scott decision of 1857 seen as a victory by slave states over use of the federal government power to restrict the expansion of slavery

- Secession crisis of 1860–1861

Complexity point

- Compare the states' rights arguments of the 1820 to 1860 period with the concern over creating a strong central government after the American Revolution as illustrated by the Articles of Confederation.

- Discuss how the appropriate role of the central government was debated in the 1960s and 1970s in the civil rights movement and how it became an issue in the rise of the Conservative movement in the late twentieth century.

4. Evaluate the causes that led some Americans to question the appropriate role of the central government in protecting individual rights between 1950 and 1980.

Thesis and Contextualization

During and after World War I and World War II, many African Americans migrated to the North and took manufacturing jobs there. Blacks joined the military in the 1940s, fighting the "Double V" campaign against German tyranny abroad and racial discrimination at home. The race issue in the United States became a national issue and not one existing primarily in the South. At the end of the war, President Harry Truman included civil rights for blacks in his Fair Deal domestic program, and he integrated the U.S. armed forces by executive action. In the 1950 through 1980 period, the role of the federal government to protect rights of blacks, women, and other groups led to political debate. Some believed that the central government was extending its power too far in its actions to protect individual rights.

Evidence, Analysis, and Reasoning

The following examples may be included but are not limited to:

- Beginnings of the modern civil rights movement after World War II with events such as the integration of the armed forces, integration of sports, the Montgomery Bus Boycott

- Involvement of the federal government in the civil rights movement: *Brown v. Board of Education*; federal troops into Little Rock, Arkansas, to enforce school integration

- Growing opposition to the use of federal authority

- More federal actions in favor of civil rights in the 1960s: Civil Rights Act of 1964, Voting Rights Act of 1965, President Lyndon Johnson's Great Society

- Growing opposition to the increased role of the federal government: George Wallace's candidacy for president in 1968 and 1972; challenges to government enforcement of integration in the South and elsewhere claiming the government was exceeding its constitutional powers

- Rise of the Conservative movement in the late 1960s and through the 1970s challenging the role of the federal government: Barry Goldwater's candidacy for president in 1964; the rise to prominence of Ronald Reagan and his calls for limiting the role of the federal government

Complexity point

- Compare the role of the central government in the post–World War II period with the role of the central government during the Great Depression of the 1930s.

- Discuss the ways that the Conservative movement sought to reduce the power of the national government in the 1980s and beyond.

INDEX

INDEX

INDEX

INDEX